ISLAM

CONTEXT AND COMPLEXITY

PAUL STENHOUSE is a Catholic priest, of the Congregation of the Missionaries of the Sacred Heart of Jesus of Issoudun, France. Editor of *Annals Australasia*, his translations of the *Kitāb al-Tarīkh* of the Samaritan priest Abū al-Fath, and the *Futūḥ al-Ḥabasha* by Shihab ad-Din Ahmed bin 'Abd al-Qader, were published in 1986 and 2003 respectively. He is author of monographs on Middle Arabic grammar, Samaritan history, chronology of the Samaritan High Priests and Samaritan religion.

ISLAM

CONTEXT AND COMPLEXITY

PAUL STENHOUSE

PAMPHLETEER

Pamphleteer is an Australian Scholarly imprint.

First published 2019 by
Australian Scholarly Publishing Pty Ltd
7 Lt Lothian St Nth, North Melbourne, Vic 3051
Tel: 03 9329 6963 / Fax: 03 9329 5452
enquiry@scholarly.info / www.scholarly.info

ISBN 978-1-925801-89-7

Cover design: Wayne Saunders

Contents

Preface

This series of articles on Islam appeared first in *Annals Australasia* (issues January 2015 to August 2016; with the final article appearing in *Annals Australasia,* 9/10 2018). It is offered to a wider readership in the hope that it may throw some light on the background to tragic events, unfolding as we write, throughout the Middle East, Africa, Pakistan, and Central and Southeast Asia, as well as in the USA, Europe, the UK and Oceania.

I am a Catholic priest who has been writing on the subject of Islam and associated topics for over fifty years. The greater part of my academic life has not been devoted to a study of Islam, but to a study of extant Arabic and Hebrew literature of the Samaritans. During the long period of my involvement with Samaritan history and traditions, the intellectual and literary paths I trod were continually crisscrossed by Islam and its Qur'ān, along with Islamic Law and Islamic history.

One could not fail to notice and compare the reality of Islam as I encountered it in its historical context, with the political and religious reality of Islam presented by Islamic authors, and intended for Islamic readers, or for non-Muslim readers with no experience of living under Islam to draw upon.

That Islam is not homogeneous is a given. Its complexity, however, is bewildering for non-Muslims, most of whom know little or nothing of Islam, and generally – like Pope Francis – see it as the peace-loving religion that it is proclaimed to be by many

Muslims. Others find this claim difficult to accept in the light of the wholesale destruction, and inhuman violence and cruelty perpetrated in the name of Allah by Muslim fighters against innocent fellow-citizens who are not Muslims, as well as against many of their fellow Muslims.

Too many Western politicians, journalists, academics, religious and cultural leaders were unprepared for the global chaos that has resulted from fatally flawed decisions concerning Islam and Middle Eastern countries and peoples taken by the US and other Western governments over many past decades.

It is hoped that these reflections, offered in good faith, will contribute to a greater, more realistic understanding, by all concerned, of the politico-religious nature of the complex reality we know as Islam or 'Submission'. And that this understanding may lead all of us to renew our efforts to bring about harmony and lasting peace between the many branches of Islam, and between the Islamic and non-Islamic worlds.

CHAPTER 1

Christians in Pre-Islamic Arabia

Is Allah [الله] an Exclusively Islamic Word?

NOT VERY MUCH of substance has survived – independently of the Qur'ān[1] – that can throw light on many of the religious beliefs and practices of pre-Islamic pagan Arabia. From about 525 to 622 we do have preserved for us a few proverbs, certain legends and a fairly abundant amount of poetry, allegedly from this time, written down and edited by Muslim authors – but this was many years after the death of Muḥammad.[2]

> There are also a few pieces of prose, mainly legends and traditions composed in Islamic days which purport to have come from earlier times. … The Arabian genealogist like his brother the Arabian historian had a *horror vacui,* and his fancy had no difficulty in filling gaps.[3]

Of the period before Muḥammad – described as Jāhilīyya,[4] or 'Time of Ignorance,' in the Qur'ān – what was retained was only what was necessary to help make sense of references to pre-Islamic times in the Qur'ānic text, or in the accounts of Muḥammad's life. While the text of the Qur'ān is regarded as unquestionable and normative, its descriptions of Jewish and Christian beliefs are, in the words of David Margoliouth 'well-known to be gross travesties of those systems, [and] we have no guarantee that its treatment of Arabian paganism is any fairer'.[5]

A veil was thrown over the memory of pagan customs and rituals throughout Arabia, and particularly in Mecca, a hot and barren sanctuary with its Ka'aba, where Muḥammad was born, and fertile Yathrib (to be known as Medīna an-Nabī, 'city of the prophet') where, in 622, Muḥammad, then Emir, made his home, gained supporters and later died in 632.

Christians in Mecca

A similar veil obscures for most Muslims the significant Christian presence and practice in Arabia during the alleged Jāhilīyya, before the birth of Muḥammad around 570.

Large numbers of Christian tribes – the Kalb, Tamīmi, Taghlibi,[6] Ayyūbi and many others like the Banu Nājiya – are known to have inhabited or moved around vast areas of Arabia in pre-Islamic times.[7]

Christian and Jewish communities of physicians, musicians and merchants were to be found in Mecca even several generations after Muḥammad,[8] and Christian and Jewish Arab tribes had been doing business in Arabia for centuries. The Christian tribe of the Banu Ghassan, for instance, even had a stall close to the Ka'ba in Mecca because they were ḥulafā', 'associates' of the Christian Quraish clan of Banu Assad.[9]

Another Christian tribe, the Banu 'Ijl of Yamama in central Arabia and Hira in Mesopotamia, had their representative in Mecca from the Banu Bakr bin Wa'il tribe – Furat ibn Hayyan – who was ḥalif or 'associate' of the Quraish clan of Sahm.[10]

Non-Muslims Banned from Using Arabic 'Muslim' Terms

How thoroughgoing this ignorance of a pre-Islamic Christian presence in Arabia is among our region's Muslim populations was borne out by recent revelations that ten of Malaysia's thirteen states had banned Catholics and other non-Muslims from using up to thirty-five Arabic terms that had entered the Malay language.

Terms banned include the word *Allāh*, 'God,' *solat* (*sic*) 'prayers,' and even *masjid* 'mosque'. In the Malaysian state of Selangor, non-Muslims are barred from using twenty-five words either orally or in writing according to the *Non-Islamic Religion Enactment 1988*. Among these banned words are *Allāh*, 'God,' *Firman Allāh,* 'Allāh's decree,' *solat* (*sic*) 'daily prayers,' *rasul,* 'apostle,' *mubaligh* 'missionary,' *mufti,* 'Qur'ānic lawyer,' *iman* 'faith,' *Kaabah*, 'Sanctuary of the Sacred Stone,' *Qiblat* 'direction in which Muslims pray' and *Haji* 'A Muslim who has made the pilgrimage'.

Selangor has also banned non-Muslims from using ten other phrases, among them *subhan Allāh*, 'Praise God,' *insya-Allāh* (*sic*), 'If God wishes,' and *Allāhu akbar* 'God is the greater' orally or in writing.

'Those found guilty of using such terms can be fined up to RM3,000 or jailed for up to two years, or both. Similar enactments are found in nine other states but not in Sabah, Sarawak, Penang and the Federal Territory. Malacca, which does not have a sultan, has banned more words and phrases than most states.'[11]

Use of 'Allāh' [الله] by Christians before Islam Arose

Those responsible for all the foregoing enactments, and for the ban on the use of 'Allāh' by Catholics sanctioned by the Federal Court of Malaysia only recently, seem to be unaware of this centuries-old presence of Christian tribes speaking Aramaic and Arabic in Arabia before Islam arose. The blanket media coverage of the horrific violence in Iraq, Syria, Afghanistan and throughout the Middle East and Africa, and the targeting of Christian minorities there, makes this ignorance difficult to comprehend.

The claim that 'Allāh' is exclusively an Islamic word ignores the fact that Muḥammad's father's name was 'Abdullah – 'Servant of Allāh'. He was not a Muslim. He died before Muḥammad was born; and depending on which year you take Muḥammad to have been born, 'Abdullah was either seventeen or twenty-two years old when he died in 570, fifty-two years before the Hijra – Muḥammad's fleeing from Mecca to Yathrib/Medina – which marks the beginning of the first year of the Islamic era (A.H.).[12]

The Christian theologian Origen Adamantius (writing sometime before 240) says in the Introduction to his edition of the Hexapla, or the Bible in six translations, that he had also looked at an Arabic translation, presumably on one of his three visits to the Province of Arabia during the first half of the third century. Nothing more is known of this. It is thought to have been in Nabataean, and written using Nabataean script – for Arabic cursive script had not yet been developed.[13]

North western Arabia – modern-day Syria and Jordan – was ruled by the ancient Arab Nabataean kingdom which had a trading network centred on oases that it controlled from the Euphrates to the Red Sea.

A Christian Arab, Marcus Iulius Philippus, known as 'Philip the Arab,' became emperor of Rome in 244. He was born in 198 in a village now called Shuhba on the road from Damascus to Bostra, the ancient Nabataean capital in southern Syria, in the district of Dara'a.[14]

Dara'a has been the scene of much death and destruction during the so-called civil war in Syria, in recent years.

Most scholars accept that in all likelihood the Qur'ān – compiled and published in the second half of the 7th century – is the earliest book written in the Arabic language.[15] The date of the oldest extant complete Qur'ān is much disputed. It varies from the middle to late 7th century to the middle of the 8th century.[16]

As for extant translations of the Bible into Arabic, all evidence points to a late 7th century date for a text of the Gospels in the Vatican Library,[17] or, with greater certitude to an 8th century origin.[18]

Another text of the Gospels in Arabic in the Vatican Library, copied in Cairo in 993,[19] always translates 'God,' and 'Lord,' as 'Allāh' [الله].

The Mt Sinai Arabic Codex 151, the oldest known *extant* copy of the whole bible translated into Arabic, also dates from the 9th century – from 867 – when, we are told, it was 'done'.[20]

Does 'done' here mean 'copied' or 'translated'? Many authors imply, and the unnamed author whom I'm quoting asserts, that this was the date of the translation. As I've not seen the colophon – the description at the end of a MS, often much ornamented, giving the copyist's name, date and place of the copying etc. – I can't verify if this date is the date the text was copied by a scribe, or the date when it was translated and written by the author.

Having worked for many years on Arabic MSS of Samaritan histories I can confidently say that it would be extremely rare to find such an original or *autograph* copy. In which case the autograph copy of Mt Sinai Arabic Codex 151 may well predate 867, and may even date from the 8th century or earlier. Whatever be the truth of the matter, in this early Arabic Bible, 'God' is always translated by 'Allāh' [الله].[21]

We know, moreover, that ninety-nine years before the Hijra – in Najran in south Arabia in what is today Yemen, many hundreds of local Christian Arabs were murdered in 523 by the Himyarite King Dhu Nuwas who had converted to Judaism. Ten of his victims were called, like Muḥammad's father, 'Abdullah – a north Arabic name used as a Christian Arab baptismal name in this south western Arabian town.[22]

One of the leading Christians murdered at that time – Abdullah bin al-Thamir – is said by Ibn Ishaq the earliest biographer of Muḥammad, to have worn a ring with a seal, inscribed with 'My Lord is Allāh' [ربي الله]. The body and the ring were discovered more than 100 years later in the time of Caliph 'Umar in the late 630s, when the ruins of Najran were being excavated.[23]

A pre-Islamic fragment of Psalm 78 (77)[24] discovered in Damascus has the Greek text on one side and the Arabic text in Greek characters on the other. In this fragment, the Greek word for *Theos* 'God' is translated into Arabic as 'Allāh' [ٱللّٰه].[25]

The earliest known and dated inscription in Arabic is on a Martyrion – a church or shrine containing the relics of a Christian martyr, St Serge – built in 512 in Zebed, south of Aleppo, Syria. Texts are in Greek, Syriac and Arabic. 'God' is translated as 'Allāh' [ٱللّٰه].[26]

Christian Cathedrals in Yemen

In addition to the Ka'aba, which as the name suggests, is the cube-shaped former pagan sanctuary in Mecca that Muḥammad made the centre of Islamic devotion and pilgrimage, there were two other Ka'abas in Arabia – one in the same city of Najran on the Sa'ūdī-Yemeni border where the Christians were killed by Dhu Nuwas, and the other in San'ā, the present-day capital of Yemen. Christian Cathedrals once stood on the sites of both these old sanctuaries.[27]

The earliest datable church to be built in the Roman province of Arabia seems to have been in Umm al-Jimal, which today is in Jordan, about 10 km from the Syrian border. It was built in 345 – two hundred and seventy-seven years before the Hijra.

The whole town was Christian and had fifteen churches from different periods, that can be seen today – all now in ruins. The name 'Allāh' was found in Umm-al-Jimāl in a pre-Islamic Christian Arabic inscription dated in the sixth century, but in the form 'Hallāh'.[28]

Of course many churches had been built before that, but not all the buildings bore a date or could be dated easily by other means.

In the third century Christians were very numerous among the Nabataeans of Idumaea. Nelson Glueck identified three hundred early Christian sites in the Negev region of today's Israel, which was then part of Idumaea.[29]

A well-known tradition speaks of a mass-movement of 30,000 'Saracens' in the Ba'albek region of modern Lebanon who became Christians at this time through the activity of a priest from Antioch called Nonnus.[30]

Bishops from Arabia at Early Church Councils

In 325 – two hundred and ninety-seven years before the Hijra – the First Council of Nicaea met not far from Constantinople. Pope Sylvester was represented by his Legate, Bishop Hosius of Cordoba in Spain. Three hundred and eighteen bishops were present of whom five were from the Roman province of Arabia as it then was: including Lebanon, Syria, Jordan, Palmyra, and Arabia proper. Among them was one, Bishop Pamphilos, of the Bedouin Arabs (Tāyyāyē) of Mesopotamia. As well, there was Bishop Petros of Aila ('Aqaba), Bishop Marinos of Palmyra, Bishop Magnos of Damascus and Bishop Kyrion of Philadelphia ('Amman).[31]

This Council defined the Divinity of Christ, the Son of God, against Arius, and fixed the manner for determining the date of Easter which Catholics still follow today. It also gave us the Nicaean Creed which we recite at Mass on Sundays and Solemnities.

In 381 – two hundred and forty-one years before the Hijra – the first Council of Constantinople met in Constantine's 'New Rome'. One hundred and fifty bishops attended, and at least four of them were from Arabia. Neither Pope Damasus I nor his Legates attended because of friction between the Emperor and the Pope. This Council defended the decrees of the Council of Nicaea against the followers of Macedonius who denied the divinity of the Holy Spirit. Pope Damasus approved only the first four canons of the Council *post factum*, and thereby legitimized it.[32]

In 431 – one hundred and ninety-one years before the Hijra – the Council of Ephesus was attended by more than two hundred bishops, at least twenty of whom came from the Province of Arabia. Pope Celestine was represented by two bishops – Arcadius and Projectus, and a Roman priest, Philip. The Council Fathers declared Mary to be the Mother of God (Theotokos) and condemned the heresy of Nestorius the bishop of Constantinople, who was excommunicated.[33]

In 451 – one hundred and seventy-one years before the Hijra – the Council of Chalcedon defined the two natures (Divine and human) of our Lord, against Eutyches, the 'Archimandrite' of a Monastery near Constantinople, who was excommunicated. 'Archimandrite' was an honorary title similar to 'Monsignor' in the Latin Rite.

Pope St Leo the Great sent legates – Bishops Paschasinus of Lilybaeum, Bishop Lucentius and two priests Boniface and Basil, and Bishop Julian of Cos – to the Council which was attended by 150 bishops including at least twenty who were from the Province of Arabia, three of whom represented nomadic Arab tribes. These latter were: John, 'Bishop of the Saracens,' named John of the Tāyyāyē; Eustathius, 'Bishop of the Saracens', one of the signatories to the letter of the Bishops of Phoenicia to Pope St Leo the Great regarding the murder of Proterius of Alexandria in 457; and John, Bishop of the Bedouin encampments in the desert between Jerusalem and the Dead Sea.[34]

Linguistic Factors Underlying Heresies

Latin and Greek were the languages of the Ecumenical Councils and of the Eastern, Byzantine Empire. By the time of Justinian (527–565) Latin had ceased to be the common tongue of Constantinople, although it was still an official language.[35] Not all who attended the Councils from the Province of Arabia and whose mother tongues were Aramaic and Arabic, however, necessarily understood clearly what was discussed, and the theological subtleties of decisions taken. Also they were culturally not always at home with the superficially more sophisticated Latin and Greek speakers.

Many of them were men of simple faith, and after the Council of Ephesus, numbers – mainly of the Western tribes – embraced Nestorianism, or what they understood as Nestorianism.

After the Council of Chalcedon in 451 some of them from the eastern tribes, with their followers, often led by personal loyalties, drifted into the Monophysite (sometimes called Jacobite) heresy – attributing only one, divine nature to our Lord, rather than two natures, divine and human, as defined by the Council.

Christian Refugees from Persia in 339

Around 339 persecution of Christians by the Zoroastrian Shapur II in Persia drove thousands of Christian refugees down the Arabian side of the Persian Gulf, preaching Christianity and establishing monasteries.

One such refugee – 'Abdisho, 'Servant of Jesus' – built a monastery around 390 on the island of Bahrain. The first known Nestorian Christian Synod was held in 410 and included delegates from Qatar and Bahrain.[36]

In the fifth century there was an extensive community of Christians mainly of the Tanukh tribe, in the Hirtha, or encampment west of the Euphrates not far from Babylon.

In the third century, when many of them were still Catholics, they had settled there following the fall of the Parthian dynasty in Persia, around 225–397 years before the Hijra. This is what is sometimes called the Lakhmid dynasty after its tribal founder. Numbers of these Eastern Tanukhs became Nestorians after the Council of Ephesus in 431.

St Moses, 4th Century Bishop of the Nomadic Arabs

The Eastern Tanukhs had connections with the Western Tanukh confederation of tribes that ranged the deserts and territories from the Euphrates to modern-day south-western Turkey.

When the sheikh of the Western Tanukh federation died around 373 his wife, Māwiyya (Maria) assumed leadership of the tribes, and bested the armies of the Arian Byzantines.[37] She fought them after they unleashed a savage persecution against Catholics, and especially the monks, in Alexandria.

Māwiyya eventually agreed to make peace with Constantinople on condition that a certain holy man, Moses, who lived in a nearby desert – probably Sinai – was consecrated bishop for her tribes. Moses refused Byzantine demands that he be ordained by their Arian bishops. They had to send him back into the desert to be ordained by exiled Catholic bishops there.

He is honoured as a saint by the Catholic Church. His feast day[38] is February 7. In 377, when Constantinople was being besieged by Goths and Huns, Māwiyya sent a troop of Arab cavalry to aid the Byzantines and this helped to raise the siege.

Two Popes Join Hands Across the Centuries

In 740 – a little over 100 years after Muḥammad's death – the Holy Father Pope Gregory III (731–741) encouraged the Wessex-born monk St Willibald to leave his Monastery of Monte Cassino near Naples and help St Boniface, who was his cousin, to evangelize the German tribes.

To inspire the young Anglo-Saxon monk Pope Gregory held up St Moses, the holy bishop of the nomadic Western Saracen tribes, who died in the fourth century, as an example of zeal and courage.[39]

In 2014 the Holy Father Pope Francis, elected in 2013 and still reigning, in order to provide spiritual care for Arabic and Aramaic speaking Chaldaean Catholic refugees from Iraq and Syria who fled to Australia, appointed His Excellency Archbishop Amel Shamon Nona, formerly Chaldaean Archbishop of Mosul in Iraq, to be Bishop of the Chaldaean Eparchy of St Thomas the Apostle, in Australia.

Māwiyya, Queen of the Arab federation of Western Tanukh Christian tribes, would have been proud.

For all its length, this too brief survey of a Christian – *Catholic* (also called 'Chalcedonian' or 'Melkite'), *Nestorian* (also called 'Church of the East') or *Monophysite* (also called 'Jacobite') – presence in pre-Islamic Arabia, has barely skimmed the surface. It offers a foretaste of what is to come in the following chapters.

CHAPTER 2

Setting the Stage for Muhammad and Islam

Mis-steps by Byzantines and Persians

IN 405 Alaric, leader of the Visigoth (Western Goth) hordes, was advancing towards Italy from the East.

Emperor Theodosius I had died in 395. Arcadius (395–408), his older son, inherited the eastern Byzantine Empire, and ruled from Constantinople; Honorius (393–423) the younger son, inherited the western Empire, and ruled from Milan, and then from Ravenna in northern Italy. Both were minors.

Honorius was under the guardianship of Stilicho, a brilliant commander who ably defended Italy against the invading Goths. The last western Emperor, Romulus Augustulus, was to die in 476. From that time the Roman Empire was ruled from the east, from Constantinople.

What if the young and inexperienced western emperor Honorius had not authorized the withdrawal of all the legions on Rome's northern border along the Rhine river in 402/403?

Having done so, in the unusually cold winter of 406 when the Rhine was deeply frozen over, hostile Germanic tribes – the Alans, Suebi and Vandals – were able to cross it, passing unchallenged by the many unmanned Roman forts.

Perhaps more to the point, what if the same emperor Honorius hadn't listened to malicious gossip from jealous courtiers and allowed his most capable general, his mentor and his father-in-law Flavius Stilicho, to be arrested and executed in August 408? Having done so, Honorius found that Stilicho's loyal troops defected in large numbers to Alaric the Visigoth, and he found himself superseded as emperor of the West by a usurper, Priscus Attalus.

Had Honorius done none of those, would Alaric the Visigoth and his horde still have succeeded in 410 in doing the unimaginable? Would they – for the first time in eight hundred years – have been able to besiege and sack *Roma Pulcherrima,* 'Rome the most beautiful,' as the poet Virgil[1] described her, and *Lux orbis terrarum et Arx omnium gentium*, 'light of the world, and refuge of all peoples,' in the words of Cicero?[2]

***

Years ago I read with interest 'If Don John of Austria had married Mary Queen of Scots' by G. K. Chesterton; and 'If Louis XVI had taken the advice of Anne Robert Jacques Turgot his brilliant Finance Minister and instituted the reforms he recommended,' by André Maurois. Both were published in 1932. Along with an article by Winston Churchill 'If Lee had not won the battle of Gettysburg.[3]

History is littered with these 'What if's.'

This is as true of the history of Muḥammad and the rise of Islam as it is of the fall of the Roman empire; or of the beheading of Mary Queen of Scots for treason; or of the fall of the Bourbons in France after more than 500 years, with the beheading of Louis XVI and Marie Antoinette.

A War to Spawn Countless Wars

In 502, war broke out between the Eastern Roman – the Byzantine – Empire and the Parthian/Sasanid Empire of Persia. Emperor Kavad I needed money to pay off the Hephthalites, known as the White Huns, who had helped him regain the throne of Persia.

When the Byzantine Emperor Anastasius I refused to pay the subsidy demanded, Kavad declared war. That war was to wage on and off for one hundred and twenty-six years.

It would prepare the way for the rise of Political Islam that, in the words of Reinhart Dozy, would unleash untold centuries of war that 'would drench Spain and Sicily, the deserts of Atlas and the banks of the Ganges with blood'.[4]

When the war between Ctesiphon, capital of the Parthian/ Sasanid empire, and Constantinople, capital of the Byzantine empire, ended in 628 both empires would be exhausted financially and militarily. Riven by internal dissension neither empire would be prepared for the fierce assaults from an unexpected quarter – nomadic Arab Muslim forces from the Hijaz in north western Arabia.

Damascus would fall in 635, and the whole of the Roman province of Syria would be lost from north to south by 636. Ctesiphon the Persian capital, and the once mighty Persian empire, would cease to exist by 637. Baghdad would be built from Ctesiphon's ruins.

Constantinople would hold on for another eight hundred years, until 1453, but by then the city of 'New Rome' built by Constantine the Great between 324 and 330, would be all that was left of the once vast Byzantine Empire.

It would be steadily gnawed away by Persians, Seljuk and Ottoman Turks, Turkomans, Huns, Vandals, Avars, Alans, Visigoths and Ostrogoths and all manner of Muslim forces. Impregnable Constantinople, the pearl in the vanished Roman empire's crown, would fall to the Turks on Tuesday 29 May 1453.

But that still lay in the future.

Byzantine and Persian Empires: What Might Have Been

In 581 Flavius Mauricius Tiberius Augustus was crowned Byzantine emperor in Constantinople. He inherited a bankrupt empire that on and off for more than a century had been obliged to pay untold thousands of pounds of gold each year to successive Parthian/Sasanian emperors of Persia as tribute for an uneasy peace between the two empires.

Then, in 590, Persian balance of power shifted. The Sasanian king of Persia Hormizd IV was deposed, blinded and killed. His son, Khosrau II, was proclaimed king in a coup organized by two of Khosrau's Parthian uncles, Vinduyih and Vistahm – his mother's brothers.

The young king was quickly deposed in his turn by his own military commander-in-chief Bahram Chobin, and fled to

Syria, or, according to some, to Constantinople, with his uncles. Against the advice of his Senate, Byzantine emperor Maurice decided to help the young Persian prince regain his throne.

In 591 a combined Byzantine-Persian army won a decisive victory over the usurper, and Khosrau II was restored to the throne of Persia in Ctesiphon. He would occupy it for the next thirty-seven years, until 628, four years before the death of Muḥammad.

So far so good. Or was it?

Khosrau II rewarded Maurice for helping him regain his empire by granting him western Armenia up to lake Van – now the largest lake in eastern Turkey – and Lake Sevan, and with a number of cities, including Martyropolis and Yerevan.

The Byzantine Empire had never been so powerful. The peace between Ctesiphon and Constantinople meant that no tribute needed to be paid. An unprecedented Golden Age seemed to be looming.

A series of regrettable and avoidable bad judgements over the next ten years by – in the words of Edward Gibbon – 'the two monarchs which balance the world; the two great luminaries by whom it is vivified and adorned,'[5] put an end to that dream. And set the stage, as we shall see, for much else besides.

Mis-steps by Emperor Maurice

For long-term security from sudden military incursions by enemies, Byzantines and Persians alike depended on friendly Arab clans whose encampments dotted the deserts and the fringes of towns and cities of both empires.

Not all Byzantine commanders were brilliant strategists like the Bulgarian-born General Flavius Belisarius who died in 565. He defeated Persians, Vandals and Ostrogoths by using military strategies employed by the Eastern Empire's fiercest enemies, the Huns and the Goths.

Few Byzantine commanders were as flexible as Belisarius. The Persians, on the other hand, were skilled in adjusting to desert conditions and cooperating with their Arab allies who knew the terrain better than they, and knew how to turn it to their advantage.

Byzantine emperors were no less clumsy than their military commanders in dealing with their Arab 'allies'.

In 573 Mundhir, sheikh of the powerful Ghassani Arab clan, learnt by chance of a plot to kill him that involved Byzantine Emperor Justin II. Mundhir renounced his allegiance to Constantinople and allowed Arab forces loyal to the Persians to attack Byzantine territory. After some time the situation was normalised, but deceit and mutual mistrust were rife.[6]

In 580, the year before he became emperor, Maurice was commander of a combined force of Byzantine and Ghassani Arab forces aiming to capture Ctesiphon. The attack had to be called off when it became clear that the Persians had been alerted to their plans. Maurice shifted blame onto Mundhir who was accused of treason, and exiled to Sicily.

Mundhir's four sons and the whole Ghassan clan responded by pillaging Byzantine towns and military settlements and laying siege to Bosra in southern Syria. Mundhir's eldest son negotiated with Maurice, and under a guarantee of safe-conduct went to Constantinople where he was treacherously packed off to join his father in Sicily.

In 599 or 600, apparently strapped for cash, Emperor Maurice refused to ransom 12,000 of his soldiers who had been captured by fierce Avars – nomadic mounted warriors of Scythian origin, cousins to the dreaded Huns. The prisoners were executed by their captors and a subsequent Byzantine military delegation to Emperor Maurice headed by an officer called Phocas was humiliated and ignored in Constantinople.

In 602, again perhaps because of lack of money to pay his soldiers, Maurice ordered the army to winter beyond the Danube. The army protested and eventually mutinied, demanded that Maurice abdicate and nominated Phocas as emperor.

Maurice fled to Chalcedon – now known as Kadiköy and only a short ferry-ride from Istanbul – and was captured. On 27 November 602, he was forced to watch five of his sons being killed before he was himself beheaded. Theodosius, his heir, who had fled towards Ctesiphon – reminiscent of youthful Khosrau II's flight in 590 – was apprehended, and then beheaded in Nicea. Maurice's wife Constantina, and her three daughters were beheaded at Chalcedon some time in 605.

Mis-steps by King Khosrau II

In the meantime in Persia, Khosrau II had grown suspicious of his conspiring uncles to whom he owed his throne. He had rewarded them with positions of power. Realising his mistake – or fearing that he had made one – he quickly had Vinduyih executed, but Vistahm rebelled in 594/5 when he heard of his brother's fate and the battle for power between nephew and uncle – actually between Sasanian and Parthian – dragged on for seven crippling years. Even after Vistahm was assassinated, his troops, like the troops of Stilicho in the time of Honorius, fought on and the rebellion was not quelled until 602.

In 602 Khosrau II miscalculated again – this time by setting a trap for an Arab ally whom he thought to be an enemy. He enticed him to Ctesiphon with a letter that said, 'the King has business with you'.[7] He arrived and was imprisoned in a Sasanian fortress at Khaniqin to the north east of Ctesiphon, where he died. This, however, was no ordinary Arab; nor was he Khosrau's enemy.

He was a powerful Arab king, Nu'man IV, who ruled the Lakhmid dynasty whose centre was Hira, on the west bank of the Euphrates, not far from Ctesiphon. His Arab subjects were mainly Christian. Since the late 4th century the clans that made up this powerful Arab kingdom had alternated between supporting the Byzantines, and the Persians in the ongoing wars between the two empires.

Nu'man had evidently refused to help the young prince Khosrau II in his fight with Bahrām back in 590 and Khosrau still nursed a grudge. He put a puppet on the throne of Hira – Iyās ibn Qabīṣa who had helped him when he was fleeing Bahrām.

Khosrau, if I may use the metaphor, had foolishly cut off his nose to spite his face. His empire would not long survive his removing the last Lakhmid king loyal to the Persian throne.

For centuries the Lakhmids had been a feared and respected buffer against nomadic Arab infiltration of Persia's borders. With Nu'man a victim of Khosrau's duplicity, Persia lost its most powerful defence on its south western flank, and would prove to be helpless against the hostile Muslim Arab forces that would build up within the next twenty-eight years in north western Arabia.[8]

When news had reached him of the coup in Constantinople, Khosrau II was probably genuinely offended by the shameful murder of Emperor Maurice and his sons in November that year. But, just as probably, was he anxious to re-possess the Armenian territory he had granted to Maurice in 591. He reclaimed that lost territory, and then his armies invaded Syria. In 608 they were heading towards Constantinople.

The Emperor Heraclius

In 610, a thirty-six-year-old soldier with red-gold hair and almost excessive personal courage – Flavius Heraclius Augustus – rebelled against emperor Phocas, killed him and was crowned Byzantine emperor.

He tried to make peace with Khosrau II but the latter had lost patience with Byzantine double-talk. He had the unfortunate ambassadors whom Heraclius sent for this purpose, killed.

Heraclius was to reign until 641. He would live to see Islam arise as self-proclaimed heir presumptive to the thrones of Zoroastrian Ctesiphon and Christian Constantinople.

But that still lay in the future.

Jerusalem Falls to the Persians

In 614 – probably in spring or summer as this was the time that ancient societies went to war[9] – the Persian army under command of General Shahrbaraz, laid siege to Jerusalem.

After twenty-one days the city fell, tens of thousands of Christians were killed, and many more thousands enslaved, many churches were destroyed, the Church of the Holy Sepulchre was set on fire, and the Holy Cross was taken to Ctesiphon as spoils of war.[10]

The Persians conquered Egypt in 618. Meanwhile the Byzantines were disrupted by internal disputes and rebellions, and were under pressure from hordes of Avars who were moving from their camps in Hungary, through Thrace, to attack Constantinople. With Palestine, Syria and Alexandria lost, Constantinople 'was hemmed in by the Mongols on the land and the Persians on the sea'.[11]

Heraclius Defeats Khosrau II

Heraclius, however, was biding his time. What seems to have re-motivated him was a blasphemous and insulting letter written by Khosrau II attacking Heraclius's honour and his faith. It was yet another of Khosrau's miscalculations. The letter was read from the pulpits of all the churches:

> You claim to put your confidence in God; then why has he not saved Caesarea, Jerusalem and Antioch from my hands? If I desire it can I not destroy Constantinople in exactly the same fashion? As for your Christ, do not deceive yourself by reposing vain hopes in Him: He was not even capable of saving Himself from the hands of the Jews who crucified Him.[12]

Between 6 April 622 – the same year that Muḥammad with some of his followers fled from Mecca to Medina – and 626, Heraclius waged a number of successful campaigns against Khosrau II.

Finally, The Byzantines moved against the Persian capital Ctesiphon in 627. After the Battle at Nineveh in December that year, Persian resistance was shattered, and Khosrau II fled to the mountains seeking help from Satraps there.

In 628 Heraclius forced the brother-in-law of Khosrau II, Parthian General Shahrbaraz, to retreat from Anatolia when the latter attempted to capture Constantinople with the help of Avar forces.

The Persian army rebelled and Khosrau was captured and imprisoned. Kavad II – Khosrau's son by the Byzantine Princess Maria, daughter of the emperor Maurice, Khosrau's former protector – proclaimed himself king of the Sasanian/Persian Empire. He ordered all his brothers and half-brothers – seventeen in all[13] – to be killed.

On the fifth day of his father's imprisonment – 25 February 628 – Kavad ordered that Khosrau be beheaded by Mihr Hurmuz whose father had been ill used by Khosrau.[14]

Pyrrhic Victory

Then Kavad II made peace with Heraclius who did not make exorbitant demands on the now dangerously unstable Persian kingdom. Kavad was to out-live his murdered father Khosrau II by only eight months, dying of the plague.[15]

By the time Muḥammad died in Medina in 632 the throne of Ctesiphon had been occupied by nine candidates, 'and the

Persian realm sank into total collapse, together with the feeble remnants of the Sasanid royal house'.[16] Anarchy and factionalism infested the Persian empire and the whole region.

The Byzantines, however, recovered all their territories as well as their soldiers who had been captured. They received war damages, along with the True Cross and other relics taken from Jerusalem in 614.[17] It was only after this victory that Heraclius and his successors adopted the official title of *Basileus* as equivalent to the Persian title *Shahanshah* which meant 'King of Kings'.

But it was too late. None of this compensated for what the long drawn-out wars had cost. It was more than a century too late for Heraclius and the Persians to take seriously what Greek King Pyrrhus of Epirus said when he was congratulated on his victory against the Romans at Asculum in Italy in 279 BC: 'Another victory like this one, and we are ruined'.[18] The Persians and the Byzantines were ruined. And an enemy was waiting in the wings to benefit from their ruin.

The Holy Cross Restored

The date of the restoration of the True Cross to the Basilica of the Holy Sepulchre is traditionally given as 14 September, 629. Heraclius bore the sacred relic on his own shoulders, and divested himself of diadem and purple – the symbols of worldly authority and power – out of respect for the holy ground which Jesus had walked, and where he died.[19]

Amid the rejoicing, storm clouds were gathering unbeknown to the exultant throng of worshippers, soldiers, diplomats and members of the Imperial Court.

In September 629,[20] while the Christian world was celebrating Heraclius's restoration of the relic of the True Cross to the Holy Sepulchre in Jerusalem, his troops beyond the Jordan were reporting that a force of 3,000 Arab warriors had easily been repelled when they entered some villages south east of the Dead Sea called Mashārif and Mu'ta, before fleeing into the desert.

It was assumed that the force had been sent to Bosra to avenge the killing by a Ghassanid tribesman Shurahbil bin 'Amr, of an envoy from a nomadic Arab chieftan. The imperial troops decided not to pursue the fleeing nomads.[21]

Had the imperial troops known that the murdered envoy was Al-Harith bin 'Umair,[22] and that he had been sent by Muḥammad bearing a letter to the Ghassani Prince of Bosra – capital of the Roman Province of Arabia, and today a town in southern Syria – inviting him to convert to Islam, would they have pursued the Arab fighters? We shall never know. But had they pursued and defeated them, the course of history would almost certainly have been changed.

Led by Muḥammad's adopted son Zaid ibn-Hārithah who was killed in the fighting, these Muslim tribesmen had been sent to avenge the killing of the envoy,[23] but also to collect coveted Mashrafīyah swords manufactured in Mashārif and Mu'ta, to be used in Muḥammad's attack on Mecca in 630.[24]

Khalid ibn al-Walid led the shattered force back to Medina where their fellow-Muslims treated them as cowards for running away.[25]

Later to be known as *Saifallah* 'the Sword of Allah,' Khalid ibn al-Walid was to lead the Muslim forces that would capture

Damascus in 635, and in 636, at the Battle of Yarmūk, would capture the whole of Roman Syria from south to north. Heraclius is supposed to have exclaimed on that occasion: 'Farewell, O Syria: and what a wonderful country this is for the enemy'.[26]

By 637 Ctesiphon had fallen, and by 647 the Persian empire would cease to exist. In 651 its last Sassanian emperor Yazdajird III, aged 27, would be slain treacherously as he fled from the Muslim army pursuing him. And emergent militant Islam – an unfamiliar power-broker on the world's political stage – confronted the ever-dwindling Byzantine empire of Heraclius.

What If ?

What if heresies like Arianism, Nestorianism and Monophysitisim had not split the unity of Christians ?

What if the words of Isaiah (58, 9–10) had been taken more to heart by the Christian rulers of the Byzantine empire, and the sheikhs and kings of the Christian Arab tribes:

> If you cease to pervert justice,
> to point the accusing finger and lay false charges,
> if you feed the hungry from your own plenty
> and satisfy the needs of the wretched,
> then your light will rise like dawn out of darkness
> and your dusk be like noonday.

CHAPTER 3

Political Islam: Beginnings

The Oath at al-Aqaba: the *Coup* at the Colonnade

If someone around 628 had dared to prophesy that within a decade some unheralded, unforeseen power from the hitherto barbarous and little known land of Arabia was to make its appearance, hurl itself against the only two world empires of the age, seize by force of arms the one – the Persian/Sasanid – and strip the other – the Byzantine Eastern Roman – of its fairest provinces, he would undoubtedly have been declared a lunatic. Yet that was exactly what happened.[1]

In this chapter, and in the chapters to follow, we shall attempt to describe how this happened. Especially do we hope to show that 'extremist' Islam that is being spread and publicised by al-Qa'eda, ISIS and the Muslim Brothers – the object of much controversy today – is the political face of Islam founded and led by Muḥammad, prince-prophet of Medina.

We are not treating here of Religious Islam – even though its foundational texts undoubtedly have an impact on its political *persona*. Religious Islam is routinely presented to us as the only face of Islam by Islamic polemicists as well as by many Western journalists and politicians via print and electronic media. Granted this, it seems timely to explore the historical background to Islam's largely unacknowledged political face.

The Oath *(bai'a)* Taken at al-'Aqaba

We need to go back to a time shortly before the Hijra – the flight of Muḥammad and Abū Bakr, his father-in-law, from Mecca to Medina which took place in September 622 – to a clandestine visit that seventy-two Muslim pilgrims from Medina paid to Muḥammad in Mecca after they had completed the pilgrimage.

The seventy men[2] and two women appear to have been the only Muslims who were part of a group of around five hundred[3] pilgrims that came to Mecca for the Hajj.[4] One of their number was the Emir of the Banu Kazraj, Sa'd bin 'Ubādah.

They met Muḥammad and his uncle al-'Abbās bin 'Abd al-Muṭṭalib at night and in secret, in a ravine near al-'Aqaba. There they took an oath of allegiance to Muḥammad that is the paradigm for the oaths of allegiance that numerous Sunni terrorist organisations have taken to the bloodthirsty self-declared Caliph of Iraq and the Levant Abū Bakr al-Baghdādi.[5]

Before the pilgrims from Medina took the oath, Abū al-Haytham asked Muḥammad 'will you perhaps return to your own people and leave us?' if they gave him their allegiance and he was victorious over his enemies. Muḥammad smiled and replied 'You are of me and I am of you. I shall fight whomever you fight and make peace with whomever you make peace with.' In a few words Muḥammad severed hitherto sacred tribal bonds, and accepted the role of ruler of Medina.

One of their number, al-'Abbās bin 'Ubādah, then asked the pilgrims from Medina:

> 'People of the Khazraj,[6] do you know what you are pledging yourselves to in swearing allegiance to this man?' 'Yes,' they said. He continued, 'In swearing allegiance to him you are pledging yourselves to wage war against all mankind.' ... They answered, 'We shall take him even if it brings the loss of our wealth and the killing of our nobles. What shall we gain for this, 0 Messenger of God, if we are faithful?' He answered, 'Paradise.' 'Stretch out your hand,' they said. He stretched out his hand, and they swore allegiance to him.[7]

It is said that Muḥammad never touched the hands of the two women who took the oath.[8]

The Islamic 'State' that emerged after this oath was taken at al-'Aqaba, and after Muḥammad had fled Mecca and had been welcomed in Medina by the Kazraj and Aws tribesmen as their prince, brought in its train holy war (*jihad*), poll tax (*jizya*), land tax (*kharaj*), tax imposed on nomadic tribes (*sadaqah*)[9] and income and wealth tax (*zakat*); tax collectors (*'ummāl / ashāb as-sadaqāt*), envoys (*rusul*), dispatches (*kutub*) and governors (*'ummāl*). It was a well-planned and well-organised political move.

The above forms of tribute, and other taxes not listed here, along with the immense booty in money, valuables and slaves obtained from war, and the complex bureaucracy of tax collectors who visited every town and encampment, and governors of provinces, and other officials set in place by Muḥammad before his death, offer a crucial key to unlocking the significance of events that are about to be described.

The Thaqīf Tribe Gives Its 'Islām'

In 631 reports by Nabataean merchants of a large Byzantine force – numbers vary from 40,000 to 100,000 – near Tabūk in northwestern Arabia just south of present day Jordan, were circulating in Medina.

These reports prompted Muḥammad to lead an army of 30,000 Muslim tribesmen to Tabūk to fight the army of Heraclius. They found no sign of a Byzantine army in the region and after waiting a few days Muḥammad and his force returned to Medina.

Even if, as some claim, the story of the Byzantine army was a myth, and the whole exercise was a show of strength aimed at intimidating uncommitted Arab tribes, the ruse worked. Muḥammad's leading this vast force to Tabūk to confront Heraclius – an event not mentioned by Byzantine chroniclers – impressed and frightened many pagan and some Christian Arab tribes, and prompted them to desert the Byzantines and join the Muslims.[10]

Among the pagan tribes that made this prudent move was the Thaqīf, the principal tribe in Ta'īf which is about 100 km southeast of Mecca.

As an example of the way the past haunts the present, it was this same locality of Ta'īf to which the surviving members of Lebanon's 1972 parliament came in 1989 to oversee the sell-out of Lebanon under pressure from Saudi Arabia, the US and Syria. Not only was Lebanon placed under Syrian 'guardianship,' the so-called Ta'īf Accord changed the original Lebanese power-sharing arrangement unique in an Arabic speaking country, and increased the power of the Sunni Prime Minister over the Maronite Catholic President.

The so-called Lebanese 'civil war' ended, but Prime Minister General Michel Aoun was forced into exile in France, and Syrian occupation and exploitation of war-weary Lebanon was to continue for another fifteen years, ending only in 2005.

To return to our topic: a deputation of Thaqīf tribesmen – some of whose descendants are still to be found in today's Ta'īf – informed Muḥammad they were ready to offer him their 'Islam' i.e. their submission, if they could keep Al-Lat, the idol of Ta'īf's principal goddess, for a further three years.

Finally it was agreed with Muḥammad that the Thaqīf did not need to pay the tithe, nor to take part in Jihad, nor to bow down at prayer, and could keep Al-Lat for one year. Muḥammad began to compose the formal agreement, hesitating as he dictated. The scribe looked at Muḥammad seeking guidance.

'Umar, Muḥammad's father-in-law and destined to become second Caliph after Abū Bakr the father of Muḥammad's favourite wife, when Muḥammad died, was a witness to this exchange.

He leapt up, drew his sword and protested at the conditions in the proposed agreement. The Thaqīf leader replied 'We are talking with Muḥammad'. Then Muḥammad said, 'No, I won't make this covenant. You must either embrace Islam unconditionally, and observe all its precepts, without exception – or prepare for war.'[11]

The Thaqīf opted for submission on Muḥammad's terms, rather than war. This was a wise choice, for the implacable 'Umar whose impassioned sword-waving circumvented the Thaqīfs' plans for a special covenant with Muḥammad, was more feared for his scourge[12] than for his sword. 'Impetuous, cruel and of great bodily strength,'[13] it was said of him that he had been known to weep once only: when he remembered how he had buried his baby daughter alive before he became a Muslim. While the grave was being dug, the little girl patted away the dust from his hair and beard. He never forgot.[14]

In the words of David Margoliouth (1858–1940), Laudian Professor of Arabic at Oxford for almost fifty years:

> The experiences of the Prophet's life, the constant bloodshed that marked his career at Medinah, seem to have impressed his followers with a profound belief in the value of bloodshed as opening the gates of Paradise. ... Those who had to deal with the Prophet or his immediate successors in Medinah had to deal with an armed camp; with a fighting force as effective as has ever been organized when fighting depended not on brain power but physical force. The Prophet rightly claims to have set a good example in resolution and contempt of danger and fatigue. But that any of the gentler virtues were cultivated does not appear; and the vices that are associated with Asiatic despotisms seem to have displayed

> themselves from the time when the despotism of Medina was founded. The Prophet's successor and bosom friend [Abū Bakr], according to the best authorities, deprived the Prophet's daughter of her property in order to avenge an insult which his own daughter had received some years before. And in general, little love seems to have been lost between the Companions of the Prophet ... the shedding of blood, indeed, became a passion.[15]

The Death of Muhammad

A number of tribes had already broken away from the Islamic State whose capital was Medina before Muḥammad, its ruler, died. Rumours of his failing health were all that it took to kindle revolts in Nejd (central Arabia) Yemama (east of the Nejd plateau) and in Yemen (southern Arabia). Rival prophets had arisen in all three regions.

As Muḥammad lay dying – from the effects of eating poisoned lamb[16] prepared by Zaynab bint al-Harith after the battle of Khaybar, according to Muslim historian Al-Tabari (839–923)[17] – the network of tribes that had sworn allegiance to him, and of others who had submitted to *dhimmi*[18] status within Muḥammad's Muslim State, was crumbling. Major bones of contention were immemorial tribal rivalries, heavy taxes, and loss of tribal authority and independence.

As well, there was hard feeling between some Ansar or 'helpers' – the Medinan tribes who welcomed Muḥammad and his teaching, especially the Kazraj and Aws, enemies of the

Quraish, Muḥammad's tribe – and the Muhajirūn, the Meccans, mainly Quraish including some of Muḥammad's kin. These had fled with Muḥammad to Medina and thought that they should have special status because of that.[19]

The Coup at the Colonnade (as-Saqīfah)

When Muḥammad died in 632, on 6 June,[20] the Ansar, the 'helpers,' met in a colonnade belonging to the Banū Sa'ida bin Ka'ab, a clan of the Kazraj. They unanimously decided to appoint Sa'd bin 'Ubāda to rule Medina after Muḥammad. They saw themselves as 'people of power and wealth, numerous and strong in resistance' with others in their 'shade and shadow,'[21] and were confident that the Ansar were most fitted to lead the complex State political apparatus with its religious face, set in place by Muḥammad.

'Umar ibn al-Khaṭṭāb got to hear of what the Medinans were up to, and went to Abū Bakr urging him to go with him to confront them because, as he said, 'even the best of them is saying: "A leader for us and a leader for the Quraish".'[22]

So Abū Bakr and 'Umar hurried to the Colonnade, and Abū Bakr addressed the gathering. What he said to the Ansar was blunt and unequivocal: 'You are the "helpers" [*wuzarā'*] – we [the Meccans] are the leaders [*umarā'*].'[23]

The Medinans, the Ansar, were not impressed. They insisted on having a leader from among their own number, letting the muhajirūn – the Meccans who had fled with Muḥammad – choose their own leader. 'Umar's response was 'Then may God kill you,' to which their spokesman replied: 'Rather may he kill you'.

At this juncture, Abū Bakr intervened and pointed to 'Umar ibn al-Khaṭṭāb and Abū 'Ubayda and told the Ansar to choose which of the two muhajirūn they wanted.

They wanted neither, but sensing the threatening mood of the opposition, they indicated that they would – grudgingly – accept, instead, Abū Bakr as Muḥammad's successor ruling from Medina. There seems little doubt that this outcome was the desired result of collusion between the triumvirate of Abū Bakr, 'Umar and Abū 'Ubaydah.

A show of strength by the Aslam, a tribe from southwest of Medina and among Muḥammad's and the muhajirūns' earliest supporters, turned the tide in favour of the Meccans. They packed Medina's streets until they had given their allegiance to Abū Bakr as Caliph. They impressed all waverers by their formidable presence; and settled the matter. 'Umar said: It was not till I saw the Aslam that I knew for sure we had won the day'.[24]

Understandably, Sa'd bin 'Ubādah – Emir of the Banu Kazraj, who had taken part in the secret pledge at 'Aqaba, had been tortured by the Meccans and was the unanimous choice of the Ansar for Caliph – was less than pleased at the manner of his defeat.

Abū Bakr and the other members of the triumvirate declared that if Sa'd did anything to disrupt the harmony of the community 'we will strike off your head'.[25] Sa'd, the faithful Emir of the Banu Kazraj, and the first person in Medina to offer refuge to Muḥammad, refused to recognize Abū Bakr as Muḥammad's successor, narrowly escaping being beheaded, and died during Abū Bakr's caliphate.

CHAPTER 4

The Apostasy Wars

Bloodbaths Over 'a Camel's Hobble'

THE 'APOSTASY WARS,' or the 'Ridda Wars,' as they are generally described, were to occupy the greater part of the two years' Caliphate of Abū Bakr. Almost all of the Arabian tribes that originally accepted Islam,[1] apart from the Quraish in Mecca and the Thaqīf in Ta'īf, had used Muḥammad's death as an excuse to refuse to pay tribute (*sadaqah*) and the wealth tax (*zakat*). They were declared to be 'apostate' (*murtadd*). The penalty for apostasy was death. They had looked on Muḥammad more as a political figure – the prince of Medina – than as a religious leader – a prophet – and when Muḥammad died they were unwilling to accept Abū Bakr as their new prince.

They had good reason for looking upon Muḥammad as a prince more than a prophet. 'Umar the second Caliph reported that Muḥammad would have someone killed for the following reasons: if somebody killed somebody unjustly; if a married person committed adultery, and if someone fought against Allah and His prophet, deserted Islam and became an apostate.[2]

Anas bin Malik reported that after eight members of the tribe of 'Ukl gave Muḥammad their Islam (submission), they then complained about living in Medina, preferring to return to their nomadic life-style. Muḥammad let them go, suggesting that they accompany one of the shepherds who looked after the Medinese camels.

When the tribesmen stole the camels and killed the shepherd, Muḥammad had the eight of them pursued and captured and brought back to Medina. He then ordered their hands and feet to be cut off, and their eyes branded with a hot iron. 'Then he abandoned them in the sun until they died'.[3]

Many of the so-called 'apostate' tribes were willing to say the ritual prayers – that is, they were willing to remain religious Muslims – if that would protect them and their families from the Muslim armies; but they would not pay the tribute. At least that was the opening gambit when delegates of the former Muslim tribes, Banū Asad, Ghatafān, Hawāzin and Tayyi' gathered in Medina to put their proposal to Muḥammad's successor, the Caliph Abū Bakr.

'God strengthened Abū Bakr's resolution in the truth,' according to Al-Tabarī's *History of Prophets and Kings*, 'and he said "If they refuse me even a camel's hobble I will wage a jihad against them for it".'[4]

And as events were to prove, he meant it.

In his letter to Khālid ibn al-Walīd, Abū Bakr ordered him, if God gave him victory, to execute every man of the Banu Hanifah – supporters of the rival prophet Musaylima in Yamama in Central Arabia – who did not have a beard, 'over whose face a razor had passed,'[5] indicating that they had renounced Islam.

This became a merciless rule of thumb for fighting the 'apostates' who refused to pay the tax even if they were willing to profess Islam to avoid being killed.

'Islam' in a religious sense meant then and still means personal *submission* to Allah; in a political and extremist sense it meant *submission* to the Islamic State (Caliphate) that enacted laws, waged war and collected taxes in the name of Allah.

That Abū Bakr's instructions were followed to the letter by all his army commanders can be judged from this overview by Reinhart Dozy of military activity against the 'apostates' in other parts of Arabia:

> Whilst the fierce Khalid was thus quenching the insurrection in Central Arabia with rivers of blood, the other generals were doing like deeds in the southern provinces. In Bahrein the camp of the Bakrites was surprised during an orgy, and they were put to the sword. A few, however, who found time for escape, reached the sea-coast and sought safety in the island of Darin. But the Moslems were soon upon their track, and slew them all. The like carnage took place in Oman, in Mahra, in Yemen, and in Hadramaut. Here, the remnant of the forces of al-Aswad, after having in vain implored the Moslem general for quarter, were exterminated; there, the commander of a fortress could only obtain as the price of surrender the promise of an amnesty for ten persons – all the rest of the garrison being decapitated; in yet

> another district an entire caravan route was for a long time rendered pestiferous by exhalations from the innumerable decaying bodies of the rebels.[6]

Inexplicably, this compelling the rebellious Muslim Arab tribes by force of arms to remain Muslim, and to pay the tribute and tax, or in the case of Christian, Jewish or pagan tribes, to submit to Allah's will as allegedly revealed to Muḥammad, or pay the *jizya* or *kharaj* as it was then known, or be killed, is usually glossed over. It is described euphemistically as 'an attempted tribal revolt,'[7] as 'the fighting after the death of the Prophet,' and 'the community under Abū Bakr affirmed its authority by military action (the "wars of the ridda"); in the process an army was created,'[8] or in a masterly understatement, 'bring[ing] back to the Islamic fold'. For instance,

> His [Abū Bakr's] first task was to bring back to the Islamic fold a number of Bedouin tribes for whom Muhammad's death triggered a return to their ancestral ways.[9]

Before Muḥammad died, another insurrection against the Muslims broke out in Yemen, in Persian controlled south Arabia, led by al-Aswad al-'Ansi, mentioned above. He was nicknamed the 'veiled prophet' because he wore a veil to hide an allegedly deformed face.[10] His real name seems to have been 'Ayhalah.[11]

In the course of attacks on supporters of al-Aswad in north western Arabia, Khālid ibn al-Walīd reached Buṭāḥ. He deployed units of his army all around, and ordered them to issue the invitation to Islam (i.e. the invitation to *submit*) and to take the invitation to whoever had not responded; 'and if he resisted, to kill him.'[12]

Abū Bakr had written a letter to all the 'apostate' tribes against whom an army was to be sent. Among other things it said,

> God guided with the truth whoever responded to him, and the Apostle of God [Muḥammad], with His permission, struck whoever turned his back to him until he came to Islam [submission] willingly or unwillingly … I have sent to you Khālid ibn al-Walīd at the head of an army of muhajirūn and Ansar … I ordered him not to fight or to kill anyone until he has invited him to the cause of God … I have ordered him to fight those who reject [the invitation] … he will not spare any one of those over whom he can prevail. He will torture them with fire, kill them by any means, and capture the women and children. The only thing he will accept from anyone is Islam [submission].[13]

In Nejd in central Arabia, Tulayḥah claimed to be a prophet like Muḥammad, and as the death of Muḥammad became known, tribes flocked to Tulayḥah's standard. His real name was Talḥah; Tulayḥah was the name he was given by the Muslims. It seems to be a play on the Arabic word for 'evil' and 'depraved'.

Many thousands died under his 'leadership'.

In what was to prove the decisive battle with the Muslim forces, he was asked, pathetically, by the trusting tribesmen loyal to him: 'What do you want us to do?' and he said: 'Whoever of you can do as I have, and save his family, let him do so' and fled with his family to Syria leaving his followers to be massacred. He waited till Abū Bakr was dead, and then submitted to 'Umar who said to him: 'You imposter – what is left of your soothsaying?' He replied, 'there is a puff or two in the bellows'.[14]

In Yamama, east of the Nejd plateau in central Arabia, a partially deaf and blind self-styled prophet and magician named Muslim bin Habib – nicknamed Musaylimah by the Muslims – had 40,000 men under his command and was wooing the tribes.

At the end of 632 not long before Muḥammad's death, Musaylimah wrote a letter to Muḥammad as if he were writing to his peer. When Muḥammad asked the messengers if they agreed with what Musaylimah wrote, they said 'yes'. Muḥammad exclaimed 'By God, were it not that messengers are not to be killed, I would have beheaded you'.[15]

Musaylimah's tribe, the Banū Hanīfa, had gathered under his standard. He was married to Sajāh, herself a soothsayer and prophetess of the Banū Tamim, and had defeated two Muslim armies before Khālid ibn al-Walīd – 'the unsheathed sword of Allah'– arrived with a third.

Many battles were fought, and thousands died on both sides. So many of the Muslims who were Qur'ān reciters were killed that the preservation of the Qur'ān – which had not yet been produced in book form – was in jeopardy.

In the final battle, thousands more died, and when the army of Musaylimah fled into a nearby garden, with a thick wall and massive gates, it became for them all a 'Garden of Death'. Of the seven thousand who entered it with Musaylimah, none survived the horrific massacre when some of the Muslims climbed the wall, found the key and threw it over to Khālid 's army.

***

I shall leave to Reinhart Dozy (1820–1883), the justly esteemed historian of Spanish Islam, the last word in this glimpse at the background to horrors that are daily unfolding in Iraq, Syria, and throughout the Islamic world as I write:

> If the Arabs were not altogether convinced by these torrents of blood that the religion preached by Mohammed was true, they at any rate recognised in Islamism an irresistible … power. Decimated by the sword, overwhelmed with terror and amazement, they resigned themselves to becoming Moslems – at least ostensibly: and the Khalif, that they might have no time to recover from their dismay, forthwith hurled them against the Roman Empire and Persia – two nations ripe for conquest, because for many years rent by intestine discord, enervated by slavery, and cankered by all the vices of decadence. Boundless wealth and vast domains compensated the Arabs for their submission to the Law of the

Prophet of Mecca. Apostasy was unknown, it was unthinkable, it meant death – upon this point the law of Mohammed is inexorable – but sincere piety and zeal for the faith were almost equally rare. By the most horrible and atrocious means the outward conversion of the Bedawin had been effected. … it was indeed all that could fairly be looked for on the part of those unfortunate people who had witnessed the death of their fathers, brothers, and children beneath the sword of Khâlid or the other pious executioners who were his rivals.[16]

CHAPTER 5

Islam, Conquest and Espansion

Coercion and Violence

In April 637, less than ten years after Heraclius the Byzantine emperor restored the relic of the true cross to the newly rebuilt Holy Sepulchre in Jerusalem, Muslim Arab forces sent by Caliph 'Umar from remote provinces in Arabia, had captured the Holy City.

Damascus had already fallen in September 635, and the Muslim armies had seized more than two-thirds of Byzantine territory by 636. They took possession of large swathes of the former Persian empire, capturing, sacking and destroying Ctesiphon its capital within fewer than two years, from 642 to 644.

Arab raids into Byzantine and Persian territory were nothing new. They had taken place on and off for centuries. These recent Muslim raids, however, seemed to have a life of their own, and their momentum showed no signs of waning. The prospect of booty was a major incentive.[1]

'Umar and his Arab forces were not unaware that the disastrous war between Persia and the Byzantine empire that ended in 628 and had lasted on and off for 126 years had left both empires exhausted militarily and economically and riven by discord among the ruling classes. Their much flaunted wealth and hapless citizenry were fruit, ripe for the plucking.

A Problem for Modern Muslims

Coercion and armed conflict or the threat of it, played a pivotal role in the rapid rise and expansion of Islam in Arabia, Syria, North Africa, Persia and Central Asia after the death of Muḥammad. This cannot be denied without denying credibility to the bulk of Islam's historical and literary heritage.

Coercion and violence run like a *leitmotif* through the Qur'ān, and through the early biographies of Muḥammad and his successors.[2]

The same is true of the various histories of early expansionist Islam especially those by Muḥammad ibn Jarīr al-Tabarī (838–923) from Tabaristan in Iran, and Aḥmad bin Yaḥya bin Jābir al-Baladhurī (died 892) also from Persia.[3]

The Muslim envoys sent to negotiate with the Persians, explaining who Muḥammad was, and what he taught, said:

> Some of us embraced Islam willingly; others as a result of coercion. ... One of the ideas that [Muḥammad] brought from our Lord was to wage war against those who were closest to us. We

> acted upon it among ourselves, and saw that there was no turning away from what he had promised us, or any revoking of it.[4]

What these envoys referred to was not just *an idea* of Muḥammad. It was a key idea; crucial to his plan to capture Mecca. Many of the *Ansar* in Medina, Muḥammad's supporters among the Medinan tribes, were linked by family ties, trade, and the ancient pilgrim traditions, to friends and relatives in Mecca. And the *Muhajirun*, the Meccan emigrants, would have found it hard to use force against and to kill their relatives who would not 'give their Islam' to Muḥammad.

Blood relationships were, for the Arabs, of all ties, the most sacred. The preaching of war as a sacred duty – jihad – sanctioned by Allah (Q22[39]; see 2[16]) gave Muḥammad the leverage he needed to prevail upon his supporters to attack their kin, the pagan Meccans. They commenced in early 623, with raids against Meccan caravans, seeking plunder, and culminating in the taking of Mecca itself in 629.

Another Side to 'Apostasy'

The so-called Wars of the Apostates, *hurūb al-ridda*,[5] were waged by Muḥammad's first successor, Abū Bakr, allegedly to force back to Islam the 'apostate' Arab tribes – 'either a small group or the whole tribe apostatized from every tribe'[6] – that objected to paying the alms tax (*sadaqah*), and the wealth tax (*zakat*) imposed by Muḥammad. After Muḥammad's death they had felt free to withhold the tax and to withdraw *en masse* from Islam.

Abū Bakr would have none of it. He needed the tax to finance his Muslim army based in Medina. 'Because of the fewness of the Muslims and the multitude of the enemy'[7] he would also eventually need to re-insert the battle-hardened warriors who were disillusioned, and had withdrawn from Islam mainly because of the tax, into the small pool of nomadic fighters who had remained Muslims after the death of Muḥammad.

Abū Bakr made it clear that he didn't care whether the 'apostates' submitted – that is gave their *Islam* (submission) – 'willingly or unwillingly' (*tau'an au karhan*); but submit they would, or face the consequences.

Some who submitted 'unwillingly' (*'alā karhin*) were among the number of those fighters who confronted the Persians. As the envoys said to Rustam, the Persian General: 'Some of us embraced Islam willingly; others as a result of coercion.'[8]

Abū Bakr was even prepared to launch a jihad or holy war against the 'apostate' Hadramis in Yemen, if they persisted in withholding the sadaqa or alms tax.[9]

Conscription for taxation and later (from 636) for military purposes, rather than conversion to Islam for their spiritual well-being, seems a more accurate description of what motivated Abū Bakr's zeal for compelling the 'apostate' nomadic tribesmen to submit, renounce their apostasy and pay their taxes; or suffer the consequences.

Philip Hitti in his *History of the Arabs* notes another motive for Abū Bakr's all-out attack on the apostates. By this show of strength he wanted to impress the Christian, Jewish and pagan Arab tribes that had withstood Muḥammad and his teaching until then, and win them over to submitting to Islam or at least accepting dhimmi status and paying the jizya or poll tax. This tax was exacted from adult male non-Muslims of military age. The jizya was a sign of a dhimmi's submission to the Islamic state and its laws.[10]

The Allure of Booty – the Spoils of War

Abū Bakr instructed Khalīd ibn al-Walīd, nicknamed 'the unsheathed sword of Allah,' to be firm:

> When you camp somewhere, make the call to prayer, and the Iqāmah [the 2nd call to prayer said in the mosque]. Then if the people make the call to prayer, and the Iqāmah, leave them be. But if they don't, then there is nothing to do but attack them. Kill them by every means, by fire or something like that. If they answer the invitation to submission [lit. to 'Islam'], then question them. If they are prepared to pay the zakat, accept that from them. If they refuse, all you can do is attack them without any more ado.[11]

The Arab military force that Abū Bakr's policy of intransigence and brutality made possible, and that his successor 'Umar unleashed with such ferocity on the Byzantine and Persian Empires subsequent to the Wars of the Apostates which ended in March 633, and the capture of Damascus in September 635, was lured mainly by the tales of booty to be had in the enemies' cities and treasuries.

The Arab raids that developed into an all-out war were not aimed principally at converting Zoroastrian Persians or Christian Byzantines, or pagan nomads to Islam. They seem to have been outlets for the warrior class of the nomadic tribes that had embraced Islam and were forbidden to fight one another.

Apart from letting off steam, the main reason for them to fight was the hope of booty to be shared among the victors who survived. As the amount of booty grew, enthusiasm for yet more war, and therefore more booty, mounted.

Some of those who protested that they would prefer the Persians to convert to Islam 'to taking your spoils,'[12] were playing the da'wa card. For the invitation to accept Islam (*da'wa*) had to be made and rejected before the killing and booty-taking could be justified.

Conversion a Threat to the Exchequer

If Christians and Jews accepted Islam, they were exempted from the jizya, the poll tax paid by dhimmis to the treasury. During the time of 'Uthman, the third Caliph in Medina, Egypt's Copts who refused to renounce their Christian faith paid twelve million dinars[13] in tribute. But by the time of Mu'awiya the first 'Umayyad Caliph in Damascus, after many Copts had become Muslims to avoid paying the tribute, the total income from Egypt fell to five million. And under 'Umar II it fell still lower.[14]

Years later, from 699 to 701, confronted by large numbers of so-called 'converts to Islam' anxious to avoid the tax, Al-Ḥajjāj bin Yūsuf, the tyrannical Governor of Kūfa in Iraq, simply changed the rules. The new Muslim converts in Iraq lost their exemption from the *jizya* tax. The importance of the tax was paramount. It took precedence over conversion.[15]

Persia on the Brink

Muslim envoys led by al-Mughirah, offered the Persians the all-too familiar options: Embrace Islam, or pay the jizya, the poll tax, or fight and be killed.[16]

> We call upon you to embrace Islam and to accept its authority. If you agree, we shall leave you alone; we shall return [to our country] and leave with you the Book of God. If you refuse, the only permissible thing for us to do is to engage you in battle unless you ransom yourselves by paying the poll tax. If you pay this, well and good; if not, then God has already bequeathed to us your country, your sons, and your property. Heed, therefore, our advice. By God, we prefer your conversion to Islam to taking your spoils, but we would rather fight you than make peace with you.[17]

The Persian General Rustam – whose counsel was spurned by his 27-year-old king Yazdagird III to whom he nevertheless remained loyal – was astute enough to identify the real reason for the hostility and the threats, among all the good ones the envoys offered. This is how he responded to the invitation (*da'wa*) extended by the envoys, according to the Persian Muslim historian Al Tabari (839–923):

> We did not treat you badly nor did we stop sharing our wealth with you [a reference to the Arab tribes that had been allies of the Persians against the Byzantines]. Time and again you were forced out of your country [and into ours] by drought and we used to provide you with supplies and send you back home. You used to come to us as labourers and merchants and we treated you well. After you partook of our food, drank our drink and rested in our shade you described this in favourable terms to your people, invited them to come and brought them to us. … I know that only greed, covetousness and privation have caused you to do this. Go back this year, supply yourselves with provisions and you can return whenever you are in need, for I have no desire to kill you.[18]

The spoils, however, were too enticing. And 'Umar would have suspected or hoped that the Persians did not have their heart in a fight. The response had already been given by his envoys: 'We would rather fight you than make peace with you'.[19]

Brave Rustam was slain, the Persian empire fell within two years (from 642 to 644), and the foolish young emperor took flight, only to be murdered ignominiously for his clothing and his jewellery in 651 by one of his own entourage, in a miller's hut in Merv, in remote Turkmenistan.[20]

Heresy, Power Grabs and Blunders

The Persians, like the Byzantines, for all their dithering and internal dissensions, nevertheless made a brave show of defending themselves. That their defences proved ineffective was due, in no small part, to the fact that their subject peoples were tempted to view the invading Muslims as liberators from centuries of Persian or Byzantine oppression, especially from excessive taxation.

By the time the Muslim armies were confronting Byzantine and Persian forces, both empires had seriously prejudiced their chances of survival.

The Byzantines especially had lost the confidence and trust of many of the Catholic or formerly Catholic Arab tribes that lived or moved along their borders, and who were their natural allies. Some of these Christian Arab tribes and their grievances were named and discussed in our second chapter.

By their harsh treatment of tribesmen who were Nestorians or Monophysites, successive Byzantine emperors, generals and patriarchs had lost any slim hope they may have had of repelling the fanatical Muslim tribesmen who made up the armies of Abū Bakr, and 'Umar.

Had Heraclius, the Byzantine emperor, followed Belisarius's example and treated these Arab tribes more justly, one can only speculate how successful his forces would have been in repulsing the Muslim invaders, as Khalīd ibn al Walīd moved into and against Roman Syria in 634.

Caesaropapism

A virulent infection that was eventually to lead the Byzantine Greeks into schism from the Catholic Church in 1054, and ultimately to destroy the Eastern Roman Empire in 1453, and that has continuing political and religious consequences in our 21st century, was what has been called 'Caesaropapism'.

This awkward word aptly describes the inordinate influence that some emperors and imperial courts exercised in matters of Faith in the eastern Catholic Church. In practice, they denied that Rome and the Pope, the successor of St Peter, had any authority or responsibility over matters of faith in the eastern Catholic Church; or that the Pope had final authority in questions of faith; or that he was acknowledged to be the final court of appeal in the east as in the west.

The authority and role of the Pope of Rome was clear enough, however, to Eustathius, Bishop of the Saracens, who was one of the signatories, along with the Bishops of Phoenicia, to a letter written to Pope St Leo the Great regarding the murder of Proterius, the Patriarch of Alexandria, in 457.[21]

It was just as clear to Bishop Dionysius of Alexandria – *patriarchs* were still in the future – who wrote two hundred years before, to Pope Xystus, in 257 bringing him up-to-date on the heresy of Sabellius in Cyrenaica, in Libya. And when, on the death of Pope Xystus, Dionysius was himself delated to Rome by St Basil and some other bishops, Dionysius showed no resentment. He accepted the Pope's right to judge him, but protested his innocence.[22] And was vindicated.

The refusal of some, not all, Byzantine emperors and patriarchs to acknowledge the primacy of Rome and the Pope in matters of faith, meant there was no brake on the madcap interference by numerous emperors, Heraclius among them, to resolve religious discord in the empire by supporting equally suspect theses, and issuing edicts that exacerbated the discord.

The discord was further compounded and the populace even more confused by Arian Byzantine emperors, heretical patriarchs of Constantinople like Nestorius, and the Monothelite Patriarch Paul II; and Constantinopolitan Archimandrites like Eutyches, with his Monophysite heresy.

No wonder that, when the integrity of the empire was threatened by a foreign army, both civil and ecclesiastical authorities in most provinces felt little or no loyalty to Constantinople, and were relieved to have seen the last of the Byzantines. Even, and at times especially, the military just faded away.

When the Byzantine garrison in Damascus abandoned them, the Damascenes capitulated. The grandfather of St John Damascene was one of the ruling class who opened the gates of the oldest occupied city in the world and accepted the terms of surrender laid down by the victorious Muslims in late 635.

The terms concluded with the following reassurance that presumably put the Damascenes' minds at rest about the newcomers' intentions: 'As long as they pay the poll tax [*jizya*], nothing but good shall befall them'.[23]

This sounded manageable; much less oppressive than the Byzantines!

CHAPTER 6

Opening the Gates to Islam

Medina's Three Jewish Tribes

When Damascus opened its gates to Abū 'Ubaidah ibn al-Jarrāh in 635, three years after the death of Muḥammad, its mainly Christian citizens agreed to pay the Jizyah or poll-tax to the Muslim conquerors.

They also agreed to accept Dhimmi (or 'tolerated minority') status, and received, in writing, guarantees of their religious freedom and political autonomy.

They little dreamt what a force they would eventually unleash on themselves and their city.[1]

Yet the seventh century Damascenes had no choice. Surrender, in order to prevent a massacre of all the inhabitants by the Muslim army, was their only realistic option. One of the commanders of the besieging Muslim forces was Khalid ibn al-Walid – nicknamed the 'unsheathed sword of Allah'.

As it was – after a six-month siege[2] – they narrowly avoided a wholesale massacre. Damascus had seven gates and while the Byzantine commander was surrendering to Abū 'Ubaidah ibn al-Jarrāh at the Jabiyah Gate in the west, Khalid ibn al-Walid was fighting his way through the Sharqi Gate in the eastern wall. The street called 'Straight' referred to in *The Acts of the Apostles* ix, 11, ran then, and still runs, between the two gates. When the two Muslim commanders met in the middle of the street Khalid insisted that he had won the city by force. Abū 'Ubaidah, for his part, insisted that the surrender be honoured.

Fortunately for the Damascenes, Abū 'Ubaidah prevailed.[3]

But as for the ambivalently phrased guarantee that the Damascenes were offered by Khalid that 'as long as they pay the poll tax [*jizya*], nothing but good shall befall them'[4] – they must have wondered what weight could be attached to it, granted the fate of the Jewish tribes in Medina who had entered into a similar non-aggression pact with Muḥammad himself.[5]

Medina's Jewish Tribes

The fate of the three Jewish tribes in Medina – the Banu Qainuqa', the Banu al-Nadir and the Banu Quraiza – would have been common knowledge throughout Arabia and beyond. It had taken four years for their fate to be settled, and the first tribe – the Banu Qainuqa' – was exiled eleven years before Damascus fell.

Before Muḥammad's flight from Mecca to Medina in 622 these three Jewish tribes and some smaller clans, constituted a powerful majority among the population of Medina – a fertile and wealthy oasis on the spice road from Yemen to Syria.

Many of the principal non-Jewish tribes in Medina, the Aws and Khazraj – originally from Yemen[6] – were employed by Jews as agricultural labourers, or as watchmen in shops and warehouses. These two Yemeni tribes, according to 'Ali Dashti, an Iranian Muslim scholar and journalist who died in 1982, were envious of their Jewish employers.[7]

'Ali Dashti notes that one of the reasons the Aws and Khazraj approached Muḥammad to be Prince of Medina, and took the oath of allegiance to him at al-'Aqaba, on the eve of the Hijra, was their desire to overcome Jewish dominance in Medina.

> As long as the Moslems were weak, no incidents arose. Not until a year and a half after the *hijra* did the Prophet Mohammad change the direction of Islamic prayer – known as the qibla – from … Jerusalem to the Ka'ba (at Mecca).[8]

Setting the Stage for Conflict

The Jewish tribes became alarmed at this change, and one of the leaders of the Banu al-Nadir – Ka'b bin al-Ashraf – unwisely approached the Quraish in Mecca for help against Muḥammad and his supporters.

The anxiety of the Jewish tribes was further heightened by raids carried out by the Aws and Khasraj led by Muḥammad, on Quraish trading caravans – especially the Muslim victory over the Quraish at the battle of Badr in March 624.

The formerly poverty-stricken Aws and Khasraj – now replete with booty – formed what Dashti called 'a strong, united front' against their former employers under Muḥammad's leadership, and the Jewish Medinans were accused of having 'infringed the contract [with Muḥammad] in various ways'.[9] The stage was being set for confrontation with them.

Fate of the Banu Qainuqa' and the Banu al-Nadir

The first of the Jewish tribes to be targeted some time after 27 March, 624, was the Banu Qainuqa' whose settlement was near the middle of the oasis of Medina.

They were goldsmiths and armourers but not agriculturalists. According to al-Tabari's *History*, Muḥammad assembled around seven hundred of the men of the Banu Qainuqa' in the market place of Medina and called on them to make their Islam (submission). They refused and rioting broke out, and they were besieged in their enclave for fifteen days.

They surrendered and only after 'Abd Allāh bin Ubayy persistently pleaded with Muḥammad for their lives, were they grudgingly – 'he was so angry they could see shadows in his face' – permitted by Muḥammad to depart, taking with them only what they could carry on camels or other beasts of burden. Almost all their possessions, including their weapons, their tools of trade, their homes and their businesses, were forfeit.[10]

This enriched the *muhajirun* or Muslim emigrants from Mecca, and the Aws and Kasraj, and filled the other Jewish tribes with deep dismay.

In 625, sometime before August, Muḥammad appealed for someone to rid him of Ka'b bin al-Ashraf from the Banu al-Nadir. Five people volunteered, including a foster brother of

Ka'b. These tricked Ka'b into leaving his fortified residence and they murdered him.[11]

Six months after the battle of 'Uhad in north western Arabia, i.e. around September 625, the Banu al-Nadir, were targeted. They were accused of trying to kill Muḥammad, and after being besieged for fifteen days, surrendered and were allowed to leave Medina with their lives and whatever they could carry on their camels except coats of mail and armour. Muḥammad took their land, all their palm trees, and coats of mail and armour.[12]

Fate of the Remaining Jewish Tribe

By 627 the only Jewish tribe of significance remaining in Medina was the Banu Quraiza. They were to come to a worse end than their exiled fellow-Jews.

After being falsely accused[13] of helping a confederation of Quraish, Bedouin and Abyssinian mercenaries who attempted to take Medina by force, and defeat Muḥammad, they withstood a siege of twenty-five days. Finally, they, too, were obliged to surrender and looked for terms similar to those that were extended to the other two tribes.

Muḥammad refused to allow them to leave with their lives, and instead, appointed as arbiter of their fate an Aws tribesman, Sa'd ibn Muadh known to be hostile to them.[14] Sa'd ordered that every adult male be executed, their women and children enslaved, and all their property and possessions divided among the Muslims.[15]

The numbers of men beheaded range from six hundred to nine hundred, depending on the source.[16] Their wealth, their wives and their children were divided among the Muslims, and Muḥammad selected one of the women of the Banu Quraiza – Rayhanah bint 'Amr bin Khunafah – as one of his concubines.

Al-Tabari, quoting Ibn Ishaq, says that the attack on the Banu Quraiza took place, either in March or late April 627. He also describes how Muḥammad ordered that trenches be dug in the ground in Medina for the bodies of the Banu Quraiza. Then Muḥammad sat down, while 'Alī his son-in-law and al-Zubair ibn al-Awam, one of his closest companions, beheaded the men in front of him.[17]

Damascus – Capital of the Islamic Empire

Within twenty-six years Damascus – the jewel in the crown of the Byzantine Empire's Syrian territory – would become the Capital of an Islamic Empire, the centre of the 'Umayyad Caliphate under Mu'awiyah, the fifth Caliph, in 661.

'Alī ibn Abī Tālib, Muḥammad's son-in-law and cousin and adopted son, the fourth Caliph or 'successor' to Muḥammad, unlike his three predecessors Abū Bakr, 'Umar, and 'Uthman, had moved the capital of his Caliphate from Medina – where Muḥammad had spent the last ten years of his life, and where he had died in 632, and was buried – to al-Kufa in Iraq.

Kufa proved to be 'Alī's bane; he was murdered there in 661 – struck down by a sword coated with poison, wielded by 'Abd al-Rahman ibn Muljam, a 'Kharijite,' one of his former supporters. 'Abd al-Rahman was one of myriad Arab warriors disillusioned by Muḥammad's son-in-law's agreeing to settle his differences with Mu'awiyah by arbitration instead of on the battlefield. All this happened in the days before Muslims split into Sunnis and Shiʻa.

In ʻAlī's day, al-Kufa, Basra and to a lesser extent Mosul were vast encampments of Islamic fighters strategically placed adjacent to the borders of the Byzantine, and the former Persian empires.

These cities still exist in modern Iraq; and still are being fought over. Following on the ill-fated US invasion of Iraq on spurious grounds in 2003, Mosul was occupied by, and Kufa and Basra were under threat from, the murderous followers of the self-styled Islamic State led by Ibrahim Awwad Ibrahim Ali Muḥammad al-Badri al-Samarrai, who now calls himself Abū Bakr al-Baghdadi.

Return of the Kharijites

Abū Bakr al-Baghdadi, leader of ISIS, and his henchmen, and his deluded and murderous young followers, are modern-day Kharijites who prefer blood-letting to arbitration. They don't understand the meaning of the word 'mercy' or 'compassion' when dealing with non-Muslims, so-called 'infidels,' or with fellow-Muslims who refuse to be conform to their puritanical regimes.

They hide their faces behind masks, and don't hesitate to shave their beards and lose themselves in crowds to avoid detection.

Jihadists from Syria, Iraq and Libya have reportedly travelled with migrants to Europe. 'It's our dream that there should be a caliphate not only in Syria but in all the world and we will have it soon, God willing.'[18]

After 'Alī's death in Kufa, Mu'awiyah transferred the Caliphate to Damascus. Moving the seat of Political Islam away from Medina and Mecca (and Kufa) meant removing it from all the tribal rivalries and vendettas infesting these places that had led to the civil war that brought Mu'awiyah and the 'Umayyad clan to power, and that ultimately led to the murder of 'Alī.

Moving to Damascus, however, did nothing to stem the killing and violence that accompanied the spread and expansion of Islam. And the 'Umayyad dynasty which was relatively broadminded and tolerant of non-Muslims in the Empire – was to be exterminated root and branch, less than one hundred years later, in a terrible bloodbath carried out in 750 by the Abbasids.

The first Caliph of the Abbasids – the new dynasty that arose from the ashes of the 'Umayyad – was Abū al-Abbās, a cousin of Muḥammad, whose preferred nickname was *al-saffāh*, 'the killer'.[19]

Violence in Context

Muḥammad, the Caliphs who succeeded him as Princes of Medina and the Arab tribesmen who fought their jihads with such reckless abandon, were children of their times and of their desert milieux and tribal and nomadic customs.

Acknowledging this as an indisputable fact helps put the violence of their eras in perspective, but as the noted Egyptian Arabist Father Samir Khalil Samir SJ comments, it also poses grave problems for 21st century Muslims – whether they live in Islamic societies or Western non-Muslim host countries that have welcomed them as refugees or migrants.

Violence was definitely a part of the rapid rise and expansion of Islam. At the time no one found anything blameworthy in Muḥammad's military actions, since wars were part of the Arab Bedouin culture. Today the problem is that the fiercest Muslim groups keep adopting that model. They say: 'We have to take Islam to non-Muslims as the Prophet did, through war and violence,' and they base their statements on some verses of the Qur'ān.[20]

CHAPTER 7

Islam and the West

The First Five Hundred Years

CURRENT WISDOM would have it that 'five centuries of peaceful co-existence' between Muslims and Christians were brought to an end by 'political events and an imperial-papal power play,' that was to lead to a 'centuries-long series of so-called holy-wars that pitted Christendom against Islam, and left an enduring legacy of misunderstanding and mistrust'.[1]

Some years ago a school textbook, *Humanities Alive 2*, for Year 8 students in the Australian State of Victoria, carried the anti-Christian/anti-Western argument further: 'Those who destroyed the World Trade Centre are regarded as terrorists. ... Might it be fair to say that the Crusaders who attacked the Muslim inhabitants of Jerusalem were also terrorists?'[2]

Nor is scholarly work immune to post-Reformation spin against the Catholic Church and the Crusades. An article entitled 'Mt Sinai Arabic Codex 151' deplores what the author calls 'the polarization of Christians and Muslims ever since the Crusades 1095–1291.'[3]

The First Hundred Years

Muḥammad died in Medina on 8 June 632. The first of the eight Crusades to free the Holy Places in Palestine from Muslim control, and offer safe passage to the Holy Land for Christian pilgrims, was called only in 1095. The period in question is 463 years; and those years were – indisputably – not characterized by 'peaceful co-existence,' nor by absence of polarization between Christians and Muslims.[4]

For the Christian states bordering the Mediterranean, it was a 463 year nightmare: a period of regular, disorganized (and occasionally well-organized) bloody incursions by Muslim – mainly Arab and Berber – land and sea forces. These came intent on booty – gold, silver, precious stones and slaves – on destroying churches, convents and shrines of the so-called 'infidels,' and on the spread of politico-religious Islam throughout Europe from their bases in the Mediterranean and the Adriatic.[5]

At the time of Muḥammad's death there were flourishing Christian and Jewish communities in Arabia, and throughout the major centres of the Persian Empire. The whole of the Mediterranean world on its European, Asian and African sides, was predominantly Christian.

It had taken only a few years for Muslim tribesmen from Arabia, inspired by Muḥammad's example and the promise of booty, to invade the Eastern Roman or Byzantine Empire whose emperors devoted more time to religious disputation than to defending their empire.

In 633 Mesopotamia fell.[6] Within eleven years the entire Sasanid Persian Empire fell to the marauding Arab tribesmen who drove the twenty-seven-year-old Persian emperor Yazdagird, into the farthest reaches of his empire, where he was eventually murdered in a miller's hut in Merv, an oasis city in Turkmenistan.[7]

Damascus fell in 635, and Jerusalem capitulated five years after Muḥammad died, in February 638.[8]

The fall of Alexandria in 643 sounded the death knell of Hellenic civilization that once enriched the whole of the Near East with its scholarship and culture. Henri Daniel-Rops claims that from the point of view of the history of civilization, Alexandria's fall was as significant as the fall of Constantinople to the Turks eight-hundred years later.[9]

Cyprus fell in 648–9,[10] and Rhodes was pillaged in 654.[11] By 698 Carthage had fallen, Tangiers fell in 708 and by then virtually the whole of North Africa was controlled by Muslims.

Less than eighty years after Muḥammad's death, in 711, Muslims poured across the strait of Gibraltar into Spain. By 721 this Arab-Berber horde had overthrown the ruling Catholic Visigoths and, with the fall of Saragossa, set their sights on southern France.

By 720 Narbonne had fallen. Bordeaux was stormed and its churches burnt down by 'Abd al-Rahman ibn 'Abdullah al-Ghafiqi in early spring 732. A basilica outside the walls of Poitiers was razed, and 'Abd al-Rahman headed for Tours which held the body of St Martin, who died in 397, apostle and patron saint of the Franks.

'Abd al-Rahman was to be defeated and killed by Charles Martel and his Frankish army on a Saturday in October, 732, one hundred years after Muḥammad's death, on the road from Poitiers to Tours – a defeat that was hailed by Edward Gibbon and others as decisive, in turning back the Muslim tide from Europe.[12]

Muslims Forces Attack Italy

Attacks on France, however, continued, and in 734 Avignon was captured by an Arab force and Lyons was sacked in 743.[13] It wasn't until 759 that the Arabs were driven out of Narbonne. Marseilles was plundered by them in 838.

Muslim incursions into Italy had been a feature of life from the early 800s. The islands of Ponza, off Gaeta, and Ischia, off Naples, had been plundered, and then, in 813 Civitavecchia, the port of Rome, whose harbour had been constructed by Trajan, was sacked by the Arabs.

In 826 the island of Crete fell to Muslim forces which used it as their base until 961. From around 827 they then began incursions into Sicily. They took Palermo in 831, captured Messina and controlled the Strait of Messina by 842, and finally took the island in 859, after Enna (Castrogiovanni) fell to them. Syracuse, however, withstood a long siege and fell only in 878.

In 836 the Neapolitans self-interestedly invited the Muslim forces to help them against the Lombards and set the stage for more than a century of Muslim raids along the Adriatic, involving the destruction of Ancona, and Muslim progress as far as the mouth of the Po.

'Saracen Towers,'[14] south of Naples, built in the ninth century to warn locals of the approach of Arab fleets from Sicily and North Africa, still charm visitors to the Neapolitan coast.

Bari, now home to the relics of St Nicholas of Myra, the original 'Father Christmas,' fell to Khalfun, a Berber chieftan, by another act of treachery in 840. From 853 to 871 the notorious Muslim brigand al-Mufarraj bin Sallam, and his successor, another Berber named Sawdan, controlled all the coast from Bari down to Reggio Calabria, and terrorized Southern Italy. They even plundered the Abbey of St Michael on Mt Gargano. They claimed the title of Emir, and independence of the Emir in Palermo.

Naples herself had to beat off a Muslim attack in 837. But in 846 Rome was not to be so fortunate. On 23 August, 846, Arab squadrons from North Africa arrived at Ostia, at the Tiber's mouth. There were 73 ships. The Saracen force numbered 11,000 warriors, with 500 horses.[15]

Tombs of Sts Peter and Paul Desecrated

The two most revered Christian shrines outside the Holy Land, the tombs of Saints Peter and Paul, were desecrated, and their respective Basilicas were sacked, as was the Lateran Basilica, along with numerous other churches and public buildings.

The very altar over the body of St Peter was smashed to pieces, and the great door of St Peter's Basilica was stripped of its silver plates. Romans were desolated and Christendom was shocked at the barbarism of the Muslim forces.

Three years later Pope Leo IV (847–855) formed an alliance with Naples, Amalfi and Gaeta, and when a Saracen fleet again appeared at the mouth of the Tiber in 849, the Papal fleet joined forces with its allies and they repelled the Muslim fleet which turned, and ran into a violent wind-storm that destroyed it.

Survivors were brought to Rome and put to work helping to build the Leonine Wall around the Vatican. Twelve feet thick, nearly forty feet in height and defended by forty-four towers, most of this wall, and two of the round towers, can be seen still by visitors to the Vatican. These defensive walls were finished and blessed by Pope Leo IV in 852.

Taranto in Apulia was conquered by Arab forces in 846. They held it until 880.

In 870 Malta was captured by the Muslims. In 871 Bari, the Saracens' capital on mainland Italy, was recaptured from the Muslims by Emperor Louis II, who in 872 was to defeat a Saracen fleet off Capua.

At this point in our examination of the 'peaceful coexistence,' which is made much of by Muslim apologists, we are still 223 years away from the calling of the first Crusade. Perhaps readers may better understand, now, why Emperor Louis II, grandson of Charlemagne was absolutely convinced, in the ninth century, of the need for armed resistence. 'He was quite sure that Islam must be driven right out of Europe.'[16] But still there was no call for a Crusade.

Attacks on Catholics in the East

I haven't written yet of Muslim attacks against the Byzantine Empire even though these played a significant part in setting the stage for the Crusades. The much vaunted military might and political power of the eastern Roman Empire carried with it responsibility for protecting the West from Muslim invaders. This it generally failed to do.

Constantinople had been attacked in 673, and then for the next five years Arab armies and fleets attempted unsuccessfully to break through the Byzantine defences. 'Greek Fire,' a mysterious substance that burned on water, the ancient precursor to modern napalm, destroyed the Muslim fleets and won the day for the defenders.

Then, in 717, the Muslims returned to the attack, emboldened by their successes in Spain. Fate intervened, and like Charles Martel and his Franks at Poitiers in 732, emperor Leo the Isaurian (717–740) turned back the Muslim tide. Constantinople was saved – for a time. Leo, for all his military skills, was a usurper, and an iconoclast. Despite defeating the Muslims, his policies ultimately further weakened both the western and eastern Roman Empires.

In 870, when Bernard the Wise from Brittany wanted to visit Palestine he had to obtain a *laissez-passer* from Muslim authorities in Bari, on the Adriatic Coast.[17]

Attacks from the Mediterranean Continue

In 873 the Muslim forces devastated Calabria in southern Italy to the point that it was reduced to the state 'in which it had been left by the Great Flood' and the Saracens expressed their intention of destroying Rome, the city of the 'Petrulus senex,' 'the ineffective old man, Peter'.[18]

In 874 Pope John VIII did all he could to dissuade Amalfi, Naples, Benevento, Capua, Salerno, and Spoleto from forming a pragmatic alliance with the Saracens. Amalfi, Capua and Salerno alone heeded his pleas for Christian solidarity.

From the close of 876 Pope John VIII had been sending letters in all directions to obtain help against the Arab forces which were devastating southern Italy and even threatening Rome itself. He sought the aid of Duke Bosone of Milan whom

Emperor Charles the Bald had appointed his legate in Northern Italy – to no avail.

He wrote for cavalry horses to Alfonso III, king of Galicia in Spain; and for warships to the Byzantines, and from 876 until May 877 he sent numerous letters to the Frankish Emperor begging him to aid the Catholics in Italy.

The Emperor proved to be a frail reed, and in 879, upon his death, the Duke of Spoleto turned on the Pope. John VIII, unable to cope with both Saracens and Spoleto, at once, had to pay tribute of 25,000 *mancuses* annually to the Arabs. This situation lasted for two years.

In 881 the Muslim allies of the Neapolitans captured the fortress on the Garigliano, the ancent Liris, 14 km east of Gaeta close to Anzio, just north of Naples, and plundered the surrounding countryside with impunity for forty years.

Returning from a synod at Ravenna in February 882, Pope John VIII found, as he put it, that 'the Saracens are as much at home in Fundi [close to Rome, in Latium] and Terracina' (80 km SE of Rome) as in North Africa. 'Though we were seriously unwell,' wrote the elderly Pope, 'we went forth to battle with our forces, captured eighteen of the enemy's ships, and slew a great many of their men'.[19] Six hundred captives of the Saracens were liberated.

Syracuse fell to the Muslims in 878 after a nine-month siege from which few escaped alive. The Byzantine city was pillaged and destroyed. Its collapse freed-up more numerous bands of marauding Muslims to harry the Italian towns and cities.

The year 880 saw victory over Saracen forces at Naples by Byzantine Commanders and also the arrival, in waters off

Rome, of warships sent by the emperor Basil to give the Pope the means of defending 'the territory of St Peter'.[20]

Meanwhile, the Saracens had turned their attention again to southern France and northern Italy. They had taken Avignon in 734 and Marseilles in 838 and they were ravaging Provence and North Italy from their bases in the Alps. The most important of these bases was Fraxineto or Fréjus, not far from Toulon, which they captured in 889.

They were displaced temporarily from their base in 942 by Hugh of Arles who had a Byzantine fleet harry them from the sea, while he attacked from land. Horace Mann, author of *The Lives of the Popes in the Early Middle Ages (539–1304)* comments[21] that it is symptomatic of the kind of pragmatic leaders who controlled the destiny of Europe at that time, that instead of wiping out this bloodthirsty band of Muslim invaders, Hugh allowed them to stay where they were on condition that they did all they could to prevent his rival as 'king of Italy,' Berengerius Marquis of Ivrea, from returning to Italy.

The latter managed to return from Germany to Italy in 945, and the Muslims were not to be expelled completely from their lair until 972 – almost one-hundred years after capturing Fraxineto – by a league of Italian and Provençal princes.

In the meantime they infested the passes of the Alps, robbing and murdering pilgrims on their way to Rome. In 921 a large band of Englishmen, on pilgrimage to the tombs of the Apostles in Rome, were crushed to death under rocks rolled down on them by Saracens in the passes of the Alps.[22]

Still 174 Years to the First Crusade

At this point in the alleged peaceful co-existence between Muslims and Christians, we are still 174 years away from the calling of the first Crusade to free the Holy Places.

Meanwhile, Muslim fleets sacked and destroyed Demetrias in Thessaly, Central Greece, in 902, and Thessalonica the second city of the Byzantine Empire fell to them in 904. Muslim armies took Hysela in Carsiana in 887, and Amasia, the metropolitan city of Pontus in Asia Minor.

The bishop of Amasia, Malecenus, wanted to ransom those of his people who had been captured but knew that the Byzantine Emperor Leo VI would not help; so he appealed to Pope Benedict IV in Rome.

The Pope received him kindly, and gave him an encyclical letter addressed to all bishops, abbots, counts and judges and to all orthodox professors of the Catholic faith asking them to show Malacenus every consideration, and to see him safely from one city to the next.

In 905 Pope Sergius III helped Bishop Hildebrand of Silva Candida restore some of the damage done to his See by the ravaging Saracens who had devastated the Church of Silva Candida in the neighbourhood of Rome.

In 915 Pope John X successfully created a Christian League with the help of Byzantine Admiral Picingli and his fleet. Even the bickering princes of southern Italy joined forces against the Saracens, along with King Berengarius and his armies from North Italy. The enemy were holed-up in their fortresses on the Garigliano near Gaeta, north of Naples. After three months of blockade, they tried to fight their way out only to be repelled by a victorious Christian force.

In 934 the Fatimid imam al-Ka'im planned an audacious invasion of Liguria led by Ya'kub bin Ishaq. The latter attacked Genoa that year, and took it in 935.

It wasn't until 972 that Duke William of Provence succeeded in driving the Saracens finally from the fastnesses of Fraxineto. In 976 the Fatimid Caliphs of Egypt had sent fresh Muslim expeditions into southern Italy. Initially the German emperor Otho II, who had set up his headquarters in Rome, successfully defeated these Saracen forces, but in July 982 he was ambushed and his army was almost cut to pieces.

In 977 Sergius, Archbishop of Damascus, was expelled from his See by the Muslims. Pope Benedict VII gave him the ancient church of St Alexius on Rome's Aventine hill, and he founded a monastery there and placed it under Benedictine rule, with himself its first abbot.

The pontificate of Pope John XVIII (1003–1009) was marred by famine and plague and by marauding bands of Saracens who plundered the Italian coast from Pisa to Rome from bases on Sardinia.

By 1010 they had seized Cosenza in southern Italy. Then Sardinia fell to the Arabs in 1015, led by a certain Abu Hosein Mogehid (thus the Latin Chronicles). I take this person to be Mujahid bin 'Abd Allah whom Arab sources credit with the invasion.

The Saracen force based on Sardinia over the next few years torched Pisa, seized Luna in northern Tuscany, and ravaged the land. Pope Benedict VIII managed to assemble a fleet and challenged the Saracen chief who turned tail and fled to Sardinia, leaving his fleet at the mercy of the papal force which was victorious.

Mujahid bin 'Abd Allah then sent the Pope a bag of chestnuts and a message that he would arrive in the following summer with as many soldiers as there were nuts in the bag. Benedict accepted the chestnuts and sent back a bag of rice: 'If your master,' he said to the astonished messenger, 'isn't satisfied with the damage he has done to the dowry of the Apostle, let him come again and he will find an armed warrior for every grain of rice'.

The Pope did not wait for an answer but carried the war into the enemy's territory. He co-opted the combined fleets of Pisa and Genoa and they sailed for Sardinia in 1017 only to find Mujahid in the act of crucifying Christians on Sardinia. The Muslim leader fled to North Africa, and Sardinia was occupied by the Pisans. Mujahid kept trying to re-take Sardinia until 1050 when he was captured by the Pisans and the island was made over to them by the Pope.

Muslims from Spain sacked Antibes in 1003. They sacked Pisa in 1005 and 1016, and Narbonne in 1020.

Sometime around 1025 Pope John XIX granted the pallium, the sign of Ecclesiastical jurisdiction, to Archbishop Peter of Gerona in northeast Spain, on condition that he redeemed Christian captives of the Saracens as he had promised the Pope when he had come on his 'ad limina' visit.

***

The 463 years that elapsed between Muḥammad's death in 632 and the calling of a Crusade to free the Holy Places in 1095 was not a time of 'peaceful co-existence' between Muslims and

European or Byzantine Christians. Nor was it, for Christians living in Muslim-occupied territories. They enjoyed 'peace' only by keeping the lowest possible profile, paying the jizya, or head-tax, and accepting non-person status in lands that had been Christian before the Muslim invaders arrived.

The new millennium saw the situation go from bad to worse. In 1009 the Fatimid Caliph of Egypt, Abu 'Alī Mansur al-Hakim, ordered the destruction of the Holy Sepulchre in Jerusalem. The edict of destruction was signed by his 'Christian' secretary ibn-'Abdun. The Muslims destroyed the Tomb of Jesus, the Dome and the upper parts of the Church until their demolition was halted by the great mound of debris at their feet. For eleven years Christians were forbidden even to visit the rubble or to pray in the ruins.

Shocked by the destruction of Christendom's holiest Shrine, Pope Sergius IV appealed for help to go to Palestine to rebuild it. His appeal fell on deaf ears.

At the beginning of the fifth century, two hundred years before Muḥammad appeared, there were seven-hundred Catholic bishops in North Africa.[23] Two-hundred of them attended the Council of Carthage in 535. By the middle of the 900s there were forty left. By 1050, as a result of 'peaceful coexistence,' there were only five left.

In 1076, before the calling of the Council of Clermont, there were only two bishops left. We learn this from a letter that Pope Gregory VII, Hildebrand, wrote to Cyriacus, Archbishop of Carthage in June 1076. As three bishops are needed for the valid consecration of another bishop Gregory asked him to send a suitable priest to Rome who could be consecrated assistant bishop, so that he, Cyriacus, and Servandus bishop of Buzea in

Mauritania, and the new bishop could consecrate other bishops for the North African Catholics.[24]

Gregory VII, on his deathbed in 1085, dreamt of forming a Christian League for defence against Islam, and said, 'I would rather risk my life to deliver the Holy Places, than govern the Universe'.[25]

It seems to have been the Seljuk Turkish capture of Jerusalem in 1076 that finally swang the balance, exhausted the patience of the European and Byzantine Catholics, and fulfilled Gregory's wish. Pilgrimage to the Holy Places had became more difficult; a poll-tax was imposed on visitors. Those who dared journey there were harassed, robbed and some even enslaved if not killed.

At the Council of Piacenza summoned by Pope Urban II and held in March 1095, Byzantine delegates emphasized the danger facing Christendom from Muslim expansion, and the hardship facing Eastern Catholics until the infidel be driven back.[26]

They repeated an appeal made by Byzantine Emperor Alexius to Robert of Flanders asking him to return to the East with some knights to assist the Byzantines in their struggle with the Muslims.

Towards the end of 1095, Pope Urban II, at another Council held at Claremont in France, took up the suggestion, and urged Europe's Catholics to 'Take the road to the Holy Sepulchre … let each one deny himself and take up the Cross'. The Assembly rose to its feet and shouted 'God wills it'.

Muḥammad died on 8 June 632. It had taken 463 years for Europe's Catholics to combine their forces and to rise up in defence of themselves and of their Faith.

CHAPTER 8

Malaysia's Dilemma

Political Islam Waiting in the Wings

AN EDITORIAL PUBLISHED in August 2008 in the *Sun Daily*, a prominent English newspaper in Kuala Lumpur[1] alerted readers to signs that Islamization in Malaysia had moved from mere exhortation and persuasion by the Malay Muslim religious authorities, to a crude enforcement of laws that prohibit Muslims from, among other things, singing and dancing – and punishing them for not praying and fasting.

Readers were reminded that Malaysia used to take pride in its multi-ethnic and multi-religious character and the co-existence that prevailed among people of various faiths.

That was before police raids on churches and temples, the end of efforts to set up an interfaith commission, the banning of the use of the term 'Allah' by non-Muslims, and the end of discussion over Article 121 (1A) of the Federal Constitution which gave jurisdiction to Shari'a Courts over matters concerning conversion to Islam.

Malaysian politicians and political parties have proved to be adept at playing the Islamic card to attract the votes of Malay Muslims – who represent more than fifty percent of Malaysia's population – whenever polls show their political support to be waning.[2]

One consequence of the political rivalry between the Pan-Malaysian Islamic Party (PAS) which wants to turn the country into an Islamic State, and the ruling Malay Party (UMNO) which is committed to promoting Malay Nationalism, and also spreading Islam, is that many Malay Muslims have become deeply conservative. Prime Minister Najib Razak was described on 24 October 2014 as having 'to walk a difficult line between appeasing conservatives, and combating extremists'.[3]

Since the 1980s, UMNO has been expanding 'the government's Islamic bureaucracy, allowing the Syariah (Shari'a) courts to have the same legal powers as civil courts, injecting Islam into the civil service and schools, and starting up Islamic banking and universities'.[4]

The Five Faces of ISIS

ISIS had been set up in 1999 by an infamous terrorist Abu Musab al-Zarqawi (from Zarqa in Jordan). Then ISIS was called *Jama'at al-Tawhid wal-Jihad,* i.e. 'The Unit for Monotheism and Jihad'. Under that name it fought in the Iraq war, and in 2004, metamorphosed into *Tanzim Qa'idat al-Jihad fi bilad al-Rafidain,* 'The organisation of the base for Jihad in Iraq, literally: *in the land of the two Rivers,*' otherwise known as *Al-Qaeda* in Iraq (AQI).

It was to have two other name changes – 'Shura Council of the Jihadists' (MSM); and 'Islamic State of Iraq' (ISI) – before, in 2013, it settled on *Ad-Dawlah al-Islamiyah fi al-Iraq wa-ash-Sham*, i.e. 'The Islamic State of Iraq and the Levant,' whence the acronym 'ISIS'.

Abu Musab al-Zarqawi was killed by a US air strike in 2006. He was notorious for his beheadings of hostages, and numerous suicide bombings of Shi'a mosques, shrines and market places. He would surely be proud of ISIS – riddled as it is with puritanical sentiments peculiar to the Wahhabis of Saudi Arabia, and with *Takfirism* i.e. accusing other Muslims of being infidels or apostates and then murdering them.

Malaysia's Sedition Act

The Malaysian government had reportedly investigated and/or charged at least thirty people with sedition, under an archaic law it had promised to eliminate, according to the Malaysian Bar Council. Most of those investigated and charged were journalists, opposition politicians, and prominent civil society activists.

The situation had become so tense for Malaysian civil society that many hundreds of Malaysian lawyers marched through Kuala Lumpur on 16 October 2014 to protest the government's use of sedition laws to stifle dissent.[5]

'The Sedition Act is a law specifically designed to shut you up,' Christopher Leong, president of the Malaysian Bar, told his colleagues. 'We have seen the unprecedented use of this Act in the last three months against students, journalists, lawyers and academics,' he added.[6]

Appeal for Rational Dialogue

Just before Christmas 2014 a group of twenty-five prominent Malays – including former secretaries-general, directors-general, ambassadors and well-respected Malay individuals – concerned over developments affecting Islam, race relations and extremist behaviour in Malaysia, issued an open letter calling for rational dialogue on the role of Islam in a constitutional democracy.

'We refer specifically,' their letter states, 'to the current situation where religious bodies seem to be asserting authority beyond their jurisdiction; where issuance of various *fatwa* violate the Federal Constitution and breach the democratic and consultative process of *shura*;[7] where the rise of supremacist NGOs accusing dissenting voices of being anti-Islam, anti-monarchy and anti-Malay has made attempts at rational discussion and conflict resolution difficult; and most importantly, where the use of the Sedition Act hangs as a constant threat to silence anyone with a contrary opinion.'

The signatories went on to remind readers that the Federal Constitution is the supreme law of Malaysia and any law enacted, including Islamic laws, cannot violate the Constitution, in particular the provisions on fundamental liberties, federal-state division of powers and legislative procedures. All Acts, Enactments and subsidiary legislation including *fatwa*, they declared, are bound by constitutional limits and are open to judicial review.

'We want,' they said, 'Islamic law, even more than civil law, to meet the highest standards of justice precisely because it claims to reflect divine justice. Therefore, those who act in the name of Islam through the administration of Islamic law must bear the responsibility of demonstrating that justice is done and is seen to be done.'[8]

'Allah' for the Exclusive Use of Muslims

On 21 January 2015 – as if the open letter referred to above had not been published – the five-man panel of Malaysia's highest civil court headed by Federal Court judge Abdul Hamid Embong, unanimously rejected the Catholic Church's application to appeal a ban on its use of the word 'Allah' in the Malay-language section of the *Catholic Herald*.

In 2009 the High Court, on the other hand, had ruled that Malay-speaking Christians had a Constitutional right to use the word which is used by all Arabic-speaking Christians, and by Christians in Indonesia and throughout the Muslim world.

The government appealed the decision on the grounds that 'Allah' was for the exclusive use of Muslims, and that allowing Christians to use it would cause confusion and religious tension.

The 2009 decision was followed by a number of attacks on churches using Moltov cocktails, rocks and paint.[9]

The Appeal Court found in favour of the government in 2013, citing, among other things, the risk of causing confusion, and jeopardising public safety.[10] And now the Federal Court of Malaysia – the highest court in the land – has unanimously rejected the Catholic Church's application to appeal for a second time against the unprecedented ban of the use of the term 'Allah' by non-Muslims.

Catholicism in Malacca

Catholic priests first arrived in Malacca in 1511. Between 1545 and 1552 St Francis Xavier lived and preached there. Nationwide, sixty percent of Malaysia's Catholics are Malay-speaking – non-Malays who use Malay as the *lingua franca* – twenty-five percent are Chinese and fifteen percent Indian, with English being spoken by at least twenty percent of all Catholics as a first or second language.[11]

On 3 January 2014, Father Lawrence Andrew, editor of the *Catholic Herald*, was burnt in effigy in front of a police station in Hulu, a district of Selangor watched by about 400 Muslim protestors.[12]

'A decision that denies Christians the right to practise their faith in the national language is a sign of intolerance and extremism in Malaysia and a denial of basic religious freedom,' said Bridget Welsh, a senior research associate at the Centre for East Asia Democratic Studies at the National Taiwan University. 'There are real tensions over basic religious rights in Malaysia.'[13]

ISIS is profiting from these tensions. A growing conservatism among Malay Muslims, and a reported reluctance on the part of state and federal politicians to confront Islamic extremism, as well as widespread use of so-called 'Social Media' – all have played into the hands of Islamic extremists.

As have comments by Prime Minister Razak to UMNO supporters on 23 June 2014 that 'when someone dares to fight to their death, they can even defeat a much bigger team.' He went on to suggest in his speech that if UMNO members were as brave as ISIS the party would be strong.[14]

Singapore's *Straits Times* quoted Ayob Khan Mydin Pitchay – Malaysian police counter-terrorism Chief – as noting that the main medium for ISIS recruitment in Malaysia is Facebook which is estimated to have 13.3 million Malaysian accounts. 'Now, in one week, you can be a member of a terror group,' commented Ayob Khan.

Thirty-seven individuals have been arrested in Malaysia, suspected of links with ISIS.[15] In 2014 police foiled ISIS-inspired Bali-style attacks on pubs, nightclubs and a Carlsberg brewery.[16]

According to *The Straits Times* seventy-one percent of all Malay Muslims (and eighty-three percent of those in their 20s) support Islamic Shari'a punishments prescribed for theft, fornication, adultery, and apostasy.

Malaysia has a 'bitter history' of home-grown militancy. The *Jama'ah Islamiah* terrorist group was set up by Indonesian imam Abū Bakr Bashir when he was in Malaysia. Part of the planning for Al-Qaeda's terrorist attacks on 11 September 2001 was carried out in a condominium outside Kuala Lumpur.[17]

Ahmad Tarmimi Maliki, a Malaysian suspected of being a member of ISIS is believed to have been the suicide bomber who killed 25 members of an Iraqi police team in May in 2014.[18]

Closer to home, on 16 January 2015, news outlets in Malaysia reported that a Malaysian suspected of leading an ISIS terror cell, had worked in Australia since 29 September 2014.

He was detained by Australian Immigration officers on 28 December, and deported to Malaysia where he was arrested. He allegedly worked with a Malaysian couple who recruited, financed and arranged for Malaysian militants to head for Syria via Australia and Turkey.

At least five Malaysian militants are thought to have been assisted by this cell to reach ISIS and Syria via Australia. The couple was deported, and arrested in Malaysia on 7 January 2015.[19]

Those who since 2011 have been cheering on the political and media pack clamouring for Bashar al-Assad in Syria 'to go,' and who welcomed the foreign 'opposition' *mujahidun* as their numbers grew into many tens of thousands, have no one but themselves to blame if the unspeakable violence and destruction – according to the UN over 191,000 deaths[20] – unleashed on Syria, and the anti-Assad polemic and propaganda that accompanied and provoked it, has prepared the ground for ISIS.

It gets worse. Now we learn that ISIS is seeking the allegiance of the *Tehrik-i-Taliban Pakistan*, and the *Baluchistan Freedom Movement*, and doubtless has its eyes on Pakistan's notoriously insecure nuclear arsenal. Six senior figures in the Pakistani Taliban have already pledged allegiance to Abū Bakr al-Baghdadi.[21]

ISIS has received the allegiance of ten other terrorist organizations with units of battle-hardened fighters: *Jund al-Khilafah*, 'Soldiers of the Caliphate,' in North Africa; *Ansar al-Shariah* (Libya); Taliban (Pakistan); *The Islamic Movement of Uzbekistan* (Pakistan's North Waziristan); *Al-Tawhid Battalion* (Pakistan, Afghanistan); *Al-Nusra* (Lebanon); *Al Qaeda in the Arabian Peninsula* (Yemen); *Ansar al-Tawhid in the Land of Hind* (India), *Ansār Bait al-Maqdis* (Sinai) and *Jund al-Khilafah* (Egypt).[22]

ISIS has proved itself to be stronger than Al-Qaeda which helped spawn it, and it is deadly serious. It means business. It is in our region. Malaysia's dilemma is our dilemma. We need to be alert before the region becomes not just 'tourist-friendly,' but also more 'terrorist-friendly' than it already is.[23]

CHAPTER 9

Islam, the Sword or the Tax

'Gentle Invitation'?

IN FEBRUARY 2015 the world's media covered the glut of mind-numbing images coming out of Libya as ISIS – their current celebrity – satisfied its hunger for blood-letting and cruelty by hacking to death and beheading 21 Coptic Christian workers.

These innocents, in the wrong place at the wrong time, were reportedly offered their lives in return for embracing Sunni Islam. They refused and were killed. All on camera.

Pope Francis declared the 21 hostages so brutally beheaded for their faith, to be 'martyrs'.[1] As did Coptic Pope Tawadros II.

Christians are declared to be 'martyrs' when they are put to death because of their Faith. They are not – as jihadists are – declared to be 'martyrs' if they die as suicide bombers or as mercenaries in the act of killing others.

In April, a video was released showing at least 16 Ethiopian Christians being shot and another 12 being beheaded by ISIS, again in Libya. In June 2015 ISIS kidnapped at least 88 Eritrean Christians trying to flee Libya by boat to Europe.

Too often one searches in vain for any sign of grief or of regret at the barbarism committed in the name of Islam, in official statements from Muftis or Councils of Imams who make much of denouncing ISIS for acting in this allegedly un-Islamic way; or for any acknowledgement that the Qur'ān, the hadith and much of Sunni understanding of Islamic history and tradition can be appealed to in the name of Islam, by ISIS and their supporters, in defence of their actions. Even when statements which attempt to strike such a balance are issued, they are sometimes poorly translated from Arabic, or poorly expressed in the vernacular of the country from which they originate, and are rarely publicised in the media.[2]

Open Letter to ISIS

On 19 September 2014 the situation changed somewhat for the better. More than 120 Muslims in positions of authority from around the world – all Sunni – signed an *Open Letter* to Abū Bakr al-Baghdadi and the followers of ISIS. The letter drew extensively from the Qur'ān, from selected passages of the Hadith and from classic Islamic texts, to rebut the ideology of ISIS. Care was taken with the translations. Some attempt was made to support the claim that ISIS was acting in an 'un-Islamic' way.

Like the gauntlet thrown at the leaders of Egypt's al-Azhar Mosque on 28 December 2014 by President Abdul Fatah al-Sisi, the letter was an unprecedented and courageous first real attempt to dissuade impressionable young Muslims from Islamic extremism.

In his address to the Sunni Muslim leaders President al-Sisi said,

> You imams are responsible before Allah. The entire world is waiting on you. The entire world is waiting for your word ... because the Islamic world is being torn, it is being destroyed, it is being lost. And it is being lost by our own hands.[3]

The *Open Letter* to Abū Bakr al-Baghdadi and those who may be tempted to follow ISIS, was written three months before this speech by the Egyptian President.[4]

Both illustrate how intricate is the bond, and yet how deep is the rift, between Religious Islam and Political Islam.

Some commentators doubt the sincerity of the Open Letter[5] because of its ambiguity and evasiveness. Despite its flaws I thought it to be a genuine first attempt publicly to confront the difficulties and contradictions that Muslims and non-Muslims find inherent in Islam's foundational texts and traditions.

The letter's very ambiguities and evasiveness highlight the dilemma facing moderate religious Muslims confronted by the inexorable and inhuman violence of ISIS and its ilk, who claim to be devout Muslims as they murder their fellow-Muslims who don't submit to them, and non-Muslims whose only fault is that they are not Muslims.

The signatories of the letter were clearly shocked 'by the spilling of Muslim blood, and taking their lives, raping their women, stealing their wealth and violating their rights.'[6]

Their letter deplored the killing of prisoners as 'heinous war crimes,'[7] specifically condemned the merciless killing of James Foley, Stephen Sotloff and David Haines,[8] and described the Arab Christians and members of other minorities as 'friends, neighbours and co-citizens'. 'They are not enemies but friends'. They deplored their being killed, their churches and other holy places destroyed, and their possessions seized.[9]

The signatories felt obliged to praise ISIS for being fearless and being ready to sacrifice their lives, but they denied that jihad could be waged 'just because people have different religions or opinions'.[10]

This is a welcome clarification. They went on to make it clear that 'jihad without legitimate cause, legitimate goals, legitimate purpose, legitimate methodology and legitimate intention is not jihad at all but war-mongering and criminality'.

But their explanation of what would be this '*legitimate* cause, *legitimate* goal, *legitimate* purpose, *legitimate* methodology and *legitimate* intention' that justifies jihad, raises more difficulties than it solves. It leaves the non-Muslim lost in a swirling mass of undefined terms and finely nuanced ambiguities that would make the Delphic oracle blush.[11]

Islam's leading historiographer Ibn Khaldun (1332–1406), in his *Muqaddimah* or 'Introduction to History,' is not so nuanced. Writing for his fellow Muslims, he did not scruple to make transparently clear that 'in the Muslim community the holy war is a religious duty because of … the obligation to convert everybody to Islam either by persuasion or by force.'

He notes that for 'other religious groups,' the 'holy war' is 'not a religious duty for them'. He explains that this is so because, for other religions, political authority and power 'has nothing to do with religion,' and he adds: these other religions are under no obligation to gain power over other nations, 'as is the case with Islam'.[12]

Dr Ibrahim Awwad al-Badri a.k.a. Abū Bakr al-Baghdadi, the self-styled 'Caliph' of the Islamic State, can be assumed to be aware of Ibn Khaldun's *Muqaddimah* and its unequivocal position on Jihad. As Ibn Khaldun's statement undoubtedly agrees with al-Baghdadi's thinking, it would have been helpful if the signatories had addressed this point.

Do they agree that Islam is obliged 'to gain power over other nations' either 'by persuasion or by force'? If they differ from Ibn Khaldun, how do they plan to counteract his influence on impressionable young Muslims likely to support al-Baghdadi and ISIS?

Islam, the Sword or the Tax

As mentioned above, their letter is unprecedented. They devote the letter to refuting ISIS's interpretation of the Qur'ān, the Hadith and Islamic tradition. Implicitly it acknowledges that there are passages in the Qur'ān, the Hadith and much of Sunni understanding of Islamic history and tradition that can be appealed to by ISIS and their supporters in defence of their actions in the name of Islam.

ISIS is criticized in the letter for giving Arab Christians and the Yazidis 'three choices: jizyah [poll tax] the sword or conversion to Islam'.

The signatories condemn at length the attitude of ISIS, and accuse it of abominable crimes. This is heartening for all fair-minded people, whether Muslim or non-Muslim, but are we to conclude that they disagree with Ibn Khaldun when he wrote:

> We do not think that we should blacken the pages of this book [his famous *Muqaddimah* or Introduction to History] with discussion of their [Christian] dogmas of unbelief. In general they are well-known. All of them are unbelief. This is clearly stated in the holy Qur'ān. To discuss or argue these things with them is not up to us. It is for them to choose between conversion to Islam, payment of the poll tax, or death?[13]

Ibn Khaldun's opinion, however, is not just his own. It reflects the content of the Hadith – collections of sayings attributed to Muḥammad or concerning him. To take only one example from al-Bukhārī's collection, we learn that al-Mughīra said to one of the commanders of the army of the Persian King Khosrau II:

> Our Prophet, the messenger of the Lord has ordered us to fight you until you worship Allah alone [i.e. become Muslims] or pay Jizya [the poll-tax].[14]

Muslim ibn al-Hajjāj al-Naīsābūrī, whose collection of Hadith is regarded, along with al-Bukhārī's, as one of the most reliable, declares:

> [Muḥammad] would say: Fight in the name of Allah and in the way of Allah. Fight against those who disbelieve in Allah. Make a holy war … When you meet your enemies who are polytheists, invite them to three courses of action. If they respond to any one of these, you also accept it and withold yourself from doing them any harm. Invite them to make their Islam [i.e. 'submission']; if they respond to you, accept their Islam from them and desist from fighting against them … If they refuse to make their Islam, demand from them the Jizya. If they agree to pay, accept it from them and hold off your hands. If they refuse to pay the tax, seek Allah's help and fight them.[15]

Al-Bukhārī (810–870), Muslim ibn al-Hajjāj (821–875) and Ibn Khaldūn al-ḥaḍrami (1332–1406) are only echoing the Qur'ān's apparently clear command:

> Wage war [قاتلوا] against those who do not believe in the Last Day, and who do not forbid what Allah and his Messenger have forbidden, nor follow the religion of truth [even if they are] the people of the Book, until they pay the jizya [poll tax] on the back of their hands,[16] as a sign of their inferiority.[17]

If these respected Islamic scholars are in error, this needs explicitly to be admitted and broadcast widely in the Muslim world. If they are not, then it is difficult to see how Sunni spokespeople can claim that ISIS is defaming Sunni Islam by their ideology and actions.

Gentle Invitation?

Ibn Isḥāq (704–c.767) wrote or dictated the earliest biography of Muḥammad. In his *Sīratu Rasūl Allāh,* 'Life of the Messenger of God,' we find that those who claim that the rejection by 'infidels' of the *da'wa,* 'invitation' to become a Muslim, is a hostile act against Islam, have the example of Muḥammad to support them.

Whatever may be the truth of Muḥammad's *da'wa* allegedly sent to Byzantine emperor Heraclius and Persian king Khosrau II, he certainly employed that ruse with neighbouring Christian Arab tribes in what is, today, Yemen.

The signatories to the letter released on 24 September 2014, make the following point:

> It is worth noting that most of the people who became Muslims throughout history did so through gentle invitation [*da'wah hasanah*] … and not through severity and coercion.[18]

This statement should be read in the light of the excerpt below, taken from Ibn Ishaq's Biography of Muḥammad:

> Then the Apostle [Muḥammad] sent Khalid bin al-Walid … to the tribe of Beni Haritha bin Ka'b in Najran *and ordered him to invite them to*

become Muslims, and to give them three days before fighting them [our italics].[19] If they agreed then he was to accept their submission from them; and if they refused he was to fight them. So Khalid set out and came to them and sent out riders in all directions inviting the people to Islam saying 'If you accept Islam you will save your life.' They embraced Islam because of the threat. ... When they came to the Apostle [Muḥammad] and he saw them he asked 'Who are these people who look like people from India?' and they replied, 'These people are the Beni al-Haritha bin Ka'b.' ... The Apostle [Muḥammad] said to them: 'Had Khalid not written to me that you had accepted Islam and not resisted, I would have tossed your heads beneath your feet.'[20]

Abū Bakr as-Siddīq (632–634), father of Muḥammad's favourite wife Aisha and therefore Muḥammad's father-in-law, was chosen as Muḥammad's successor, or 'Caliph,' when the latter died in 632.

In a letter addressed to Arab tribesmen who did not want to be Muslims, Abū Bakr described how Muḥammad dealt with this situation:

With His [Allah's] permission, the Apostle of Allah struck out at whoever turned away from Him until, willingly or unwillingly, he made his submission [Islam].[21]

Elsewhere in the same letter he wrote:

> I have sent to you someone at the head of an army of the *Muhajirun*[22] and the *Ansar*[23] and those who follow [them] in good works. I ordered him not to fight anyone or to kill anyone until he has called him to the cause of God … but I have ordered him to fight those who deny [Him] for that reason. So he will not spare any one of them he can gain mastery over, [but may] burn them with fire, slaughter them by any means, and take women and children captive.'[24] 'And the only thing that he will accept from anyone will be submission [Islam].[25]

It is true that the majority of the Christians in Arabia, Roman Syria, North Africa, Persia and Spain, remained Christians despite intolerable restrictions on their freedom, for quite some years after the Arab invasions. It is unpersuasive, however, to claim that those of them who became Muslims 'did so through gentle invitation and not through severity and coercion'.

The economic, political and social condition of non-Muslims living as *dhimmis*, i.e. as 'protected' people who paid the poll tax, cannot be construed as 'gentle persuasion' if later they became Muslims, without doing violence to the reality of *dhimmitude*. They were not second-class citizens: *dhimmis* were non-citizens.

Until the issues raised here – and they are only a few of the ones that could have been raised – are tackled and resolved, some may well conclude that the 120 signatories were not really serious about confronting the religious roots – the Qur'ān, Hadith and classic Sunni texts – of modern extremist Political Islam.

Readers could be forgiven for thinking that the signatories were addressing their letter not to ISIS and its fanatical followers, but to the West – especially to the West's media and to its political power-brokers.

To the Western media: because the media's growing reliance on Qatar's *Al-Jazeera* should sound warning bells about 'freedom of the Press': because many of them have shown themselves to be fascinated by the naked power exercised by ISIS; and because they, and the so-called 'social media,' have become complicit in the horrors infecting the region and beyond.

To Western power-brokers: because the West's military intervention will inevitably be called upon if the Sunni regimes in Saudi Arabia and the Gulf area are to be defended from ISIS, an evil *jinn* that some of them conjured up to help destroy Bashar al-Assad and the Alawites in Syria, and to help restore Sunni supremacy in Iraq and throughout the Muslim East.

***

In the 14th century Ibn Khaldun foresaw a time in a secular future, when Political Islam would survive only if its sovereignty (*mulk*) were based on rational laws that would enable citizens to leave a primitive way of living (*badāwa*) and change to a new and more civilized way of living (*hadāra*).[26]

Despite the tentative and halting nature of the steps taken by the 120 signatories, there is genuine hope that the voice of moderate religious Islam is at last beginning to be heard, and the vision that Ibn Khaldun had of the *mulk siyāsī* or 'sovereignty based on rational Law' may in some way be realized.

Egyptian President Abdul Fatah al-Sisi deserves to be heard. He had ISIS in mind, and did not mince his words, as he addressed the *ulamā* or 'learned scholars' of the Al-Azhar mosque and urged them to speak out against Islamic – mainly Sunni – extremism because, as he put it, 'the Islamic world is being destroyed, it is being lost. And it is being lost by our own hands'.[27]

CHAPTER 10

The West – Rediscovering Its Core

Grasping the Nettle, Part 1

THIS IS THE FIRST of two essays that will attempt to tackle a problem that troubles most thinking people today: Can a halt be made to the preaching of hatred and the acts of violence and inhumanity by fanatical Islamists in the name of Allah against non-Muslims, and other Muslims regarded as 'unfaithful' to Islam? This article asks whether the West is capable of learning from past mistakes, and of rediscovering what once made it resolute. Or will political correctness and relativism pursue their baneful pathological course until the West's Christian and democratic immune systems are so eroded, as to render it defenceless?

Much is made of the potential for global economic and social unrest from the millions of desperate refugees flowing into Europe from war-ravaged Syria, Iraq, the Horn of Africa, Central Africa and Afghanistan.

This is the same Europe of which Pope John-Paul II wrote in 2003:

> European culture gives the impression of 'silent apostasy,' on the part of people who have all that they need, and who live as if God does not exist.[1]

Many if not most of the refugees are Muslim, and the countries they are fleeing – along with much of the Islamic and Arab world – are infested with Islamic extremists, fundamentalists and extremists who have declared a holy war on the West.

This is not a figment of our imagination. This is a message Islamic fanatics have proclaimed, written, communicated verbally on radio and TV, on video and facebook, and written in black and white and the blood of countless Christian martyrs, and many of their fellow-Muslims. It may be politically correct to ignore it, but is it wise?[2]

Genuine refugees deserve all the sympathy and help that more fortunate countries can give. Economic migrants jumping the queue and terrorists, posing as victims, on the other hand, are a potentially serious problem for the host countries – especially countries that appear to have to have cut themselves off from their ancient Christian traditions.

In 2002, Cardinal Josef Ratzinger, the future Pope Benedict XVI, wrote that

> the question of the peaceableness of cultures, of peace in matters of religion, has … moved up to become a political theme of the first rank.

Cardinal Ratzinger was Prefect of *The Sacred Congregation for the Faith* when it published, in 2000, its ground-breaking *Declaration* on the truth of Catholicism, *Dominus Iesus,* which spoke of the unique and universal salvation brought by Jesus Christ and the Church. Reflecting in 2002 on reaction to the publication, Cardinal Ratzinger described how 'a cry of outrage arose from modern society,' and also 'from great non-Christian cultures'. *Dominus Iesus* was said 'to be a document of intolerance and religious arrogance that should have no place in the world today'.

The Catholic, Cardinal Ratzinger wrote, could only respond to this reaction by putting to such critics the question that Martin Buber put to an atheist: 'But what if it is true?'

The real problem, wrote the future Pope, 'lies in the question of truth … what meaning does belief have, what positive meaning does religion have, if it cannot be connected with truth?'[3]

Dialogue is the reasonable and wise person's preferred way of resolving disputes. But Marcello Pera, former President of the Italian Senate – putting his finger on the crux of the problem – pointed out how relativism and political correctness eliminate dialogue as an option:

> dialogue will be a waste of time if one of the two interlocutors states beforehand that one idea is as good as another.[4]

Muddying the Water

A recent statement by then US Secretary of State John Kerry is symptomatic of the malaise of political correctness and double-talk that infects the West, and hinders it from finding solutions to the complex human dilemmas facing it.

During a visit to Saudi Arabia on 23 January 2016, only a month away from the Iranian legislative elections in which hopes were pinned on the moderates and reformists headed by President Rouhani, Mr Kerry launched a verbal attack on Iran which has been making friendly overtures to the US and the West.

It should be noted that the US has not had normalized diplomatic relations with Iran for thirty-six years – since 1980 – in the aftermath of the student occupation of the US Embassy in Teheran in November 1979 and the ensuing hostage crisis.[5]

Kerry stated that the US 'remains concerned' about 'some of the activities that Iran is engaged in, in other countries,' referring, one assumes, to Iranian support for Shi'a in Syria. He then, reportedly, criticised 'Iran's support for terrorist groups like Hizbollah, its human rights record, and its development of ballistic missiles'.[6]

All this emerged during a media conference in Saudi Arabia whose anti-Shi'a paranoia lies behind much of the turmoil in the region.[7]

The Saudis are reportedly building an almost one thousand kilometre long razor-wire fence on their border with Iraq.[8] This seems to indicate that they know that they are in more danger from Sunni ISIS, than from Shi'a Iran.

Kerry's sub-text also suggests that the US remains unconcerned about Saudi activities in other countries (including, apparently, Wahhabi infiltration of US mosques); and unconcerned about Saudi Arabia's human rights record; and unconcerned about Saudi Arabia's ballistic missiles and any threat these might pose to neighbouring states.

To cap this public display of diplomatic double-talk, the Saudi Foreign Minister Adel al-Jubeir added the usual Wahhabi *mantra*: 'Iran remains the world's chief sponsor of terrorism'.[9]

The Elephant in the Room

Speaking of double-talk: who or what pressed the lever that set in motion the destabilizing of the Middle East, which has led to the potential destabilizing of Europe by millions of frightened refugees and other displaced persons inundating EU countries?

This is the 'elephant in the room' and it appears to remain shrouded in mystery. Or does it?

Hovering like ghastly spectres over the digital images of hapless refugees fleeing destroyed homes and businesses, murder and rape, are the misbegotten Western and US foreign policy decisions – for 'foreign' read 'commercial' – perpetrated on the world since, to take but one example, 29 May 1933.

That was the day when US lawyer Lloyd Hamilton on behalf of SOCAL (Standard Oil California) signed an agreement with the treasurer of the new kingdom of Arabia, Sheikh Abdullah Suleiman, acting on behalf of new King Ibn Saud – formerly the leader of a band of Islamist puritans terrorizing the Arabian peninsular – awarding exclusive rights for six decades to SOCAL to extract oil from eastern Saudi Arabia including offshore waters and islands, for £35,000 down, payable in gold, and an additional £20,000 to follow in eighteen months.[10]

What the US State Department subsequently called 'the greatest commercial prize in the history of the planet'[11] was predictably a poisoned chalice. It has locked the US, and, willy nilly, the rest of us, in a frenzied *danse macabre* with the Wahhabis, insanely swirling and twirling our way to ... 9/11, and its gruesome aftermath.

By 2011 the West had good reason to doubt the wisdom of what US Secretary of State Condoleezza Rice had called, in 2005, a US policy of 'creative chaos' for the Middle East; and even better reason to doubt the appropriateness of what, in 2006, she announced as the 'birth pangs' of 'a New Middle East'.[12]

The birth pangs to which Condoleezza Rice referred were the hundreds of Lebanese dead, and the more than half a million Lebanese refugees left in the wake of the Israeli war against Hizbollah under Prime Minister Ehud Olmert – which Hizbollah won decisively.[13]

By 2011, Libya was in chaos and Gaddafi had been killed; Yemen was – as it still is – in turmoil; Bahrain had shown its more brutal face; and the 'New Middle East' seemed like a sick joke. And, ominously, Syria had been nominated as the next domino to fall during the Arab Spring by the nameless string-pullers who were dissatisfied with the degree of 'creative chaos' achieved up till then.

Time described Condoleezza Rice's comment about 'creative chaos' as 'Diplomatic Disneyland'.[14] 'Nightmare on Elm Street' would have been closer to the truth. At least for the religious and ethnic minorities living in these regions.

It is worth recalling that in 2011 then-Secretary of State

Hillary Clinton expressed confidence that the Arab Spring would allow Washington to advance 'security, stability, peace, and democracy' in the Middle East.[15] Her confidence could not have been more misplaced.[16]

We have consistently maintained the unwisdom of further destabilising the Middle East and Central Asia by invading Afghanistan in October 2001, and by the twin invasions of Iraq in 1990 and 2003; to say nothing of supporting al-Qaeda in the so-called 'liberation' of Libya in 2011; and supporting Mohamed Morsi and the Muslim Brothers during the impeachment of Hosni Mubarak; and the horrendous ongoing holocaust in Syria.

Al-'Arabiya – the news service owned by Saudi Arabia, and propaganda rival of Qatar's *al-Jazeera* – would have us believe that the Syrian bloodbath began when 'protests erupted in Syria against the embattled leader's rule, but turned into civil war.'[17]

This smacks of a teenager's excuse: 'the car crashed' when, in reality, he crashed it. The protests did not *turn* into civil war – they were turned into civil war; and the US, the UK and the West, along with the Saudis and the usual suspects, were complicit in what has followed.

No one should be surprised that US ties with Saudi Arabia, and US and Western support for Hafez al-Assad – Bashar al-Assad's ruthless father, in his close dealings with the so-called civil war in Lebanon from 1975 to 1990, and subsequent occupation of Lebanon by Syria from 1990 until 2005 – could lead to the point at which we have arrived in late 2017.

But it still needs to be stressed – as the late Syrian Orthodox Patriarch pointed out to me in October 2012 in Lebanon – that Bashar al-Assad 'is not his father'; and that Syria in 2012 was not Syria from 1975–2005.

Turkey in the EU?

The European Union – if reports of German Chancellor Angela Merkel's visit to Turkey's Prime Minister Recep Erdoğan on 19 October 2015 are to be believed – is willing to speed-up the process by which Turks can travel to most EU countries without visas, and even to fast-track Turkey's admission as a member of the EU.

This is the same Turkey whose army is the second largest in NATO. How can NATO sit comfortably with a fellow NATO member's being one of the major 'interested parties' that have laid hold of Syria, and actively contributed to the horror and hopelessness engulfing it and its citizens?

This is the same Turkey whose president Recep Erdoğan, and prime minister Davutoğlu, have been complicit in the bloody chaos that has led to the refugee crisis now facing many European countries, especially Germany.

Angela Merkel's offer referred to above, is in return for Turkey's agreeing to police its borders with EU countries more effectively, improving conditions for Syrian refugees on their own soil, and imposing restrictions on some nationals entering Turkey so freely.

If Turkey were well-disposed towards Europe, wouldn't she have taken these neighbourly steps voluntarily, without needing to be bribed by a humiliated German Chancellor coming cap in hand asking for favours?

Turkey has an estimated population of seventy-five million, with an unemployment rate of more than ten percent. If Turkey were to be admitted as a member of the EU, Europe's population would grow instantly by seventy-five million, ninety-eight percent of whom would be Muslim: forty-five million Sunni, twenty-five million Alevi – a Sufi-like sect of the Shi'a – and three million Shi'a.

If Turkey were to be admitted as a member of the EU, 'Europe' would have a common border with Georgia and Armenia which may well benefit all concerned; but is Europe prepared to have a common border with Iraq, Iran and Syria?

The Tainted Fruit of Political Correctness

The EU, like the West in general, would need to be better prepared than it is, if it is to protect itself from the inevitable and profound social, economic, political and cultural changes that usually follow mass migrations of people.

George Weigel, depicts the dilemma facing the EU thus:

> What is happening when an entire continent, healthier, wealthier, and more secure than ever before, fails to create the human future in the most elemental sense – by creating future generations? There are obvious sociological and economic factors affecting Europe's demographic decline; might there be spiritual factors at play, too? Could Europe's disinclination to create the future have something to do with an apostasy toward the past – toward the spiritual roots of European civilization? And could that apostasy eventually threaten Europe's commitments to human rights, to equality before the law, to tolerance and civility among peoples of diverse convictions?

> Is it possible to sustain public commitments to those public goods on purely utilitarian grounds because civility and tolerance 'work better'? How can we speak of, and defend, 'universal human rights' in a cultural climate in which the very idea of 'truth' is under sustained assault?[18]

Yes – and how well prepared are host countries that don't insist that new arrivals master the language of their new homeland, and accept the democratic nature of their new country and its institutions; when refugees or migrants are free to choose not to integrate into the new society, and to set up their own ghetto-like communities within the host country.

How well prepared is the EU when politicians, police and media of host countries are frightened and bullied, and unsure of their own identity or core culture.

How well prepared are the host countries when what they principally have in common with new arrivals is digital technology – electronic gadgets, computers and computerised information systems, mobile phones and weapons skills.

When this stage is reached, the need for being better-prepared becomes more acute.

If one goes back into the past – about 450 years – a familiar picture emerges. The ambassador of the Habsburg king Ferdinand I – future Holy Roman Emperor – to the *Sublime Porte* of the Ottoman Sultan in Istanbul, was Ogier Ghiselin de Busbecq. Writing to a fellow diplomat, Busbecq says that the only thing saving Europe from conquest by the Ottomans was the threat to the Ottomans from Persia:

> On [the Turkish] side, are the resources of a mighty empire, strength unimpaired, habituation to victory, endurance of toil, unity, discipline, frugality, and watchfulness. On our side is public poverty, private luxury, impaired strength, broken spirit, lack of endurance and training; the soldiers are insubordinate, the officers avaricious; there is contempt for discipline; licence, recklessness, drunkenness, and debauchery are rife; and worst of all, the enemy is accustomed to victory, and we to defeat. Can we doubt what the result will be? Persia alone interposes in our favour … but Persia is only delaying our fate; it cannot save us.[19]

As it happened, Europe's political future proved to be less grim than Busbecq predicted. His fears, however, were not unfounded, and Europe's Catholic and genuinely humanistic roots have been seriously eroded as the Reformation, Enlightenment and successive revolutions ran their course.

Power and booty, rather than converting Christians or Jews to Islam, was the Ottoman motivation. And the Ottomans – provided the Christians, Jews and other minorities kept a low profile and paid their taxes promptly – would undoubtedly have employed their much feared Janissaries to defend the *dhimmis* – the 'tolerated' peoples – from the violence of the mob, in their planned European provinces, just as they did in the Ottoman Empire itself.[20]

Listing Some of the Fruits of PC

In a book published in 2006,[21] former President of the Italian Senate, Marcello Pera – an atheist – brought the focus 450 years into the present.

He described the fibre of the West as permeated 'by a mixture of timidity, prudence, convenience, reluctance and fear.'

He went on to deplore in the West what he called 'the form of self-censorship and self-repression that goes by the name of political correctness.'

Political correctness, Pera explained, 'is the newspeak that the West uses nowadays to imply, allude to, or insinuate – rather than to affirm or maintain.'

> The world is filled with concern, but also with hypocrisy on the part of people who see no evil and speak no evil to avoid becoming involved; who see no evil and speak no evil to avoid appearing rude; who proclaim half-truths and imply the rest, to avoid assuming responsibility. These are the paralysing consequences of political correctness.
>
> Whenever a culture lacks or flatly rejects our institutions we are not allowed to say that our own culture is better or simply preferable. The only thing that politeness allows us to say is that cultures and civilizations are different.

In a later book, published in 2011,[22] Pera comments:

> The main flaw of liberalism today is that it has retreated into a solely political and procedural dimension and has forgotten that it is also a tradition with a rich, specific ethical content rooted in European and American history – a history of which Christianity is an essential part. Modernity has resisted and waged war against the Church, while feeding abundantly on its Christian heritage. Its very exaltation of the individual pays secular homage to the Christian message that man was created by God in order to discover the truth about himself and the world.

Jeopardising One's Birthright

The Greek philosopher Parmenides (born c.515 BC), or Aristotle (384–322 BC), depending on which authority you accept, tells us that Nature abhors a vacuum.

Jesus told the apostles a parable that reinforces this adage. St Luke records the story in his Gospel. A man had been possessed by an evil spirit. After the evil spirit was driven out it wandered around looking for somewhere to make its home. If the man from whom the spirit had been driven had not, in the meantime, embraced the Good, the True and the Beautiful, then the evil spirit would assuredly return – this time with seven other spirits worse than itself – and possess that man. His last state would be worse than his first.[23]

Who doesn't know that creating a political vacuum invites more strongly motivated and less politically correct protagonists, to enter the fray?

The rise of an Islamic State under Muḥammad from 622 onwards was only possible because the Byzantine and Persian empires exhausted themselves fighting each other on and off, for 126 years. They proved to be no match for what a modern Iranian commentator on the period describes as 'quite small forces of ill-armed and untrained Arabs.'[24]

The vacuum was begging to be filled.

While the US and the West have ostensibly been trying to export 'democracy' to the Middle East, they have, in the process, in Winston Churchill's words, squandered vast military resources, and poured 'armies and treasure into these thankless deserts.'[25]

The consequences of their ill-thought-out schemes have provided the world's democracies with their greatest challenge so far: how to preserve their own democratic societies – ostensibly 'free' but riddled with relativism and political correctness – while welcoming the tsunami of desperate human beings genuinely seeking to make a new home in the EU and elsewhere in the West.

These have been driven from their homelands by foreign invasions and bloody civil wars whose perpetrators managed to convince the gullible West that Islamist terror was a 'reaction' to despotism and injustice, and part of an Arab Spring, when it was this, and much more.

This should not pose an insuperable problem for a Christian and democratic West, willing and prepared to welcome genuine refugees, but also prepared to defend its Faith and democratic values.[26]

CHAPTER 11

'Don't Untune That String'

Grasping the Nettle, Part II

SHAKESPEARE (*Troilus & Cressida*, Act 1, scene 3, line 109) was, as usual, right. Untuning the string that brings harmony and order, leads only to disorder and discord which in their turn lead to chaos. When we harm another human being, when we worship power, and hate and ugliness, and destroy innocence and beauty, we destroy ourselves.

From 9 April to 15 April 2016, 154 people died in twenty-six Islamic terrorist attacks in twelve countries. There were four suicide bombings and 137 people were wounded.[1]

When the late Benezir Bhutto, Prime Minister of Pakistan, was denouncing an Islamic terrorist bombing on 25 November 1995 she remarked, 'the Muslim faith does not allow the use of violence for any reason.'

Time and again her words have been repeated, mantra-like, by Western politicians and media to prove that Islamic terrorists from Usama bin Laden and the Taliban to Abū Bakr al-Baghdadi, the self-styled caliph of ISIS, and his followers, are aberrations and distortions of Islam; not the real Islam – which, we are assured, is peaceful.

With all people of goodwill, I hope and pray that Benezir Bhutto's words prove to be true, but having puzzled my way through the myriad invitations in the Qur'ān to fight and terrorise and kill unbelievers; and having read al-Tabari's account of the Ridda (apostasy) wars before and after the death of Muḥammad; and Ibn Ishaq's description of Muḥammad's exploits as a ghāzī or warlord, I wonder that Muslim parents are not more concerned lest their impressionable children take the wrong message from these well-known Islamic writings.

The 54-year-old Pakistani mother of three who was also the first female Prime Minister of Pakistan and was at the height of her powers, was murdered on 27 December 2007 when she stood up though the sunroof of her bulletproof vehicle to wave to the crowds in Rawalpindi. Her assassin was an Islamic terrorist belonging to al-Qaeda. Twenty bystanders were murdered along with her; and another twenty died in riots that followed.

Their murderer would probably have slept soundly that night, confident that he had fulfilled his duty to fight *fī sabīl Allāh,* 'for the sake [lit. 'in the Way'] of God'.

Eight years later, during a visit to Kosovo on 17 November 2015, King Abdullah II of Jordan issued a warning to Muslims and non-Muslims alike: 'We are facing a third world war against humanity, and this is what brings us together.' He went on to say that Europe and the Islamic world are threatened by Muslims who have made themselves the 'savage outlaws of religion, devoid of humanity, respecting no laws and no boundaries' by joining ISIS, al-Qaeda and other groups that use terror in the name of Islam.[2]

Legal and Political Dithering

On my return to Australia in 1981 after having been away for five years, I found that representations on behalf of the Muslim community were being made to the Australian Government to ensure that Egyptian-born religious leader Imam Taj ad-Din al-Hilali – who was awaiting deportation for overstaying his temporary visa – not be allowed to stay in this country.

By 1986, after much legal to-ing and fro-ing, the imam had still not been deported, and Chris Hurford – the then Minister for Immigration in the second Hawke ministry – tried unsuccessfully to have him deported.

In a letter to the *Sydney Morning Herald* one member of the local Muslim community explained that 'the majority of Lebanese Muslims in Australia accept the decision of the Minister for Immigration to expel the Imam Sheikh Taj el-Hilali. We believe the Minister acted within the law and without prejudice'.

Reference was made to the imam's 'preaching of fundamentalist ideas, especially to young people frustrated by lack of employment,' and the writer went on to say that allowing him to remain in Australia 'will divide the Muslim community' and 'destroy' its 'image as a useful and progressive community'.

The imam was eventually given permanent residence in 1990 by Hurford's successor in the fourth Hawke and first Keating ministry, Gerry Hand.[3]

Following advice from his Department, Chris Hurford had suggested to members of The Lebanese Muslim Association that the Grand Mufti in Beirut, or at the Al-Azhar University in Cairo, might be of assistance in finding a successor to Imam al-Hilali if the deportation eventuated.

His suggestion was met with the following response from the Association:

> This Association and its members were surprised by the Minister's suggestion that the Australian Government might intervene in religious matters when we, as Australian Citizens, claim the right to freedom of worship as we choose fit without Governmental interference … your assumption of deciding as a Minister of the Crown, to recommend one or the other Mufti as being 'more appropriate' is a decision which we are sure you are not competent to make. … You seem to believe that the religion of Islam has a hierarchical concept of priesthood. Nothing could be further from the truth. The Grand Mufti of Cairo and Beirut are Moslem Jurists who are employed by the Government on issues regarding Islamic doctrine. Although highly learned, these Jurists have no real influence, in the countries in which they reside, over any

> lesser ranking order of priests [*sic*] ... in the religion of Islam, priesthood is forbidden.[4]

Assumptions

The Australian Government and its respective departments – whose principal prior experience of dealing with migrants to Australia from the Middle East would most likely have been with Arabic speaking Christians or Jews who over many years had integrated into Australian society without losing their cultural and linguistic links with their homelands, or abandoning their religious faith – seems to have assumed, in the 1970s and 1980s that Islam was a religion more or less like Judaism or Christianity; and that Muslim migrants could be expected to integrate just as smoothly as had their Jewish and Christian co-nationals. They were seriously mistaken.

Surely it is the responsibility of government prudently to inform itself about the social, political, religious and economic background and expectations of all migrants coming to this country before they arrive, or if that is not possible, upon arrival.

Australia should have been better prepared to welcome and cushion the culture shock of the new arrivals who were Muslim. As things turned out, the culture shock-waves have also affected the non-Muslim Australian majority, whose best interests appear not to have been always well served by their government or its agents.

For most of these Muslim migrants it would probably have been their first exposure to a non-Muslim country other than through the medium of TV and the occasional letter or phone call from friends or relatives.

For centuries, the only Muslims who moved out of the *Dar al-Islam*, or Realm of Islam, or even around it, were diplomats and other government officials, and traders and merchants. Most of the Muslim population lived out their lives in secure and familiar surroundings, and were discouraged from travelling into the *Dar al-Harb* or Realm of War that is the Realm of the so-called 'infidels'.

Some would have had no idea how life in a democracy would differ from the life they had lived in their former home country whose rule would, customarily, have been despotic.

Many who had been brought up strictly would be apprehensive at the thought of living in a pluralist and secular society where religion is separate from the state. The very terms 'pluralist' and 'secular' would probably have been unfamiliar to many of them.

They would also have found it very difficult to accept the civil and secular nature of Authority and Law in their new country.

Islam – which means *submission* to God – is not just a religion; it embraces the whole spectrum of life: political, social and religious, and implies submission to those who wield authority in the name of God in all these areas; but not submission to the authority of non-Muslims.

Imam al-Hilali alluded to this question of the authority of non-Muslims over Muslims, during prayers in the Lakemba Mosque on 8 February, 1985. The official translation is clumsy but the drift is clear:

> Faithfulness should not be for a land or a government which is not Islamic; and those who

> do not share these principles are not for us, but for them.[5]

The Real Picture

Yet, at the same time, we are constantly being told by Muslim spokespersons and non-Muslim media and public figures, that the very word 'Islam' means 'peace' implying that it is by definition a peaceful religion. No Arabic dictionary confirms this claim. Two meanings only are usually given for اسلام 'Islam,' viz: 'submission,' and 'the religion of Islam'. Though سلم 'silm' a word that does mean 'peace,' sometimes is used for 'the religion of Islam'.[6]

Islam, however, does not mean 'peace,' and while one sympathises with peace-loving Muslims for wishing that it did, pretending that it does helps no one, and perpetuates a myth that obfuscates what is really at issue: the profound influence exerted by sections of the Qur'ān and the Sunnah – Islam's religious patrimony – on the bloodletting and cruelty and chaos that fills the world's TV and social media.

The preachers of hate, operating not just on the sidelines as some would have it, but in the very heart of many Islamic and some western countries, including the US, are drawing their energy from these revered sources which are readily accessible to all.

An article on deradicalisation of Muslim youth by Emeritus Professor Clive Kessler that was published in *Annals* in 2015, made the point that among Muslims worldwide today, from 10 to 15% is estimated to be reform-minded and democratic; perhaps another 10 to 15% is militant and extremist, and the remaining 70% represent what may be called conventional or quasi-traditional Islam.[7]

Professor Kessler then asks how the mainstream majority relates to the radicals and extremists. Are they opposed, or are they basically identical, or at least complementary?

According to Kessler, the Muslim mainstream, like the extremists, adheres – explicitly or by unreflecting habitual assent – to the same underlying propositions that constitute the extremist and militant world view. Like the extremists they hold, as Qur'ānic teaching has held from the outset, that Islam embodies all that was once good in Judaism and Christianity and therefore those forerunners are now superfluous and lacking in spiritual value and authenticity.

> The implication is clear. Since the extremists and the mainstream share – if in different forms and style and emphasis – the same religiously grounded historical world view, the two orientations are basically complementary and congruent, not opposed. So there is no ground within the mainstream for calling back the deviant minority; no distinctive standpoint, authentic and authoritative, to which the extremists may be called to return by abandoning their own identifiable heresies. The moderates from the centrist mainstream stand bereft of the religiously based political and moral authority to make such calls persuasively, in ways that may prove enduringly convincing.[8]

A Way Out

People of good will need to help Islam extricate itself from the historic and politico/religious labyrinth in which it finds itself: where militant Islamic extremists of whatever ilk incite religious hatred and violence against fellow Muslims who dare to criticise them, and against all non-Muslims, while quoting verses from the Qur'ān and claiming to be modelling themselves on Muḥammad.

In August 1983, President Numeiri of Sudan had imposed Shari'a on his country. In December the following year Mahmoud Mohamed Taha, an Imam from Omdurman, who was leader of the Republican Party which had sought independence from the British – gained in 1956 – was at the same time attempting to introduce a different way of viewing Islam and the Qur'ān in order to bring justice and freedom to all Sudanese.

He also wanted his teaching to provide Muslims world-wide with an escape from the tyranny of historical Islamic Shari'a. As he put it '... the fact that Shari'a does not treat women and non-Muslims equally with male Muslims, is beyond dispute'[9].

Mahmoud reminded his fellow Muslims that when Muhammed was in Mecca he preached friendship and tolerance over the thirteen years that he spent in his hometown, attempting to win over Jews, Christians and pagans to his new religion. He preached equality and individual responsibility between all men and women without distinction on grounds of race, sex or social origin. *Jihad* was not preached, nor was inequality between men and women, nor was the *hijab* required. Polygamy was not permitted: 'marriage was between one man and one woman, without dowry and without divorce.'[10]

The following verse (Q16[125]) is one of a number of so-called verses of *persuasion* that belong to the Meccan period. There are no verses of *persuasion* from the Medina period.

> Propagate the path of your Lord in wisdom and peaceable advice, and argue with them in a kind manner, your Lord is more knowledgeable of those who stray from his path and he is more knowledgeable of the guided ones.

When he found himself mocked, and his teaching rejected, Muhammed and his followers fled in 622 to Medina, an oasis 450 km away, inhabited by Jewish tribes and some Arab tribes hostile to the Meccans. He was invited by Medinan Arab tribes to become their Emir or Prince. He willingly assumed this role and the tone of his preaching changed dramatically.

After his arrival in Medina we find the verses of peaceful persuasion abrogated and verses of *compulsion* substituted. The following so-called 'verse of the sword' (Q9[5]) is typical of the verses to which I referred above:

> When the four forbidden months are over, kill the polytheists wherever you find them, and seize them and besiege them and lie in wait for them in every ambush. But if they repent and perform prayer and pay the poor-tax, then let them go their way. God is forgiving, merciful.

What is known as *Shari'a* today, and what has been criticised as incompatible with life in a modern, pluralist society, is historic Islamic Shari'a whose foundational texts are all derived from the Medina period, the last – and the most violent – ten years of Muḥammad's life.

Nevertheless, the Meccan Suras are probably the ones non-Muslims are most familiar with, because Islamic bloggers and Western media roll them out like a 'sop to Cerberus' when it is necessary to prove that Islam is tolerant and peaceful.

But they have been abrogated, haven't they? Well, not exactly. Mahmoud, quoting Q2[106] 'Whenever we abrogate a verse or postpone it,' says:

> The primary [Meccan] texts were repealed or abrogated in the sense of postponed and suspended, in relation to legislation, until their proper time, which has dawned upon us now.[11]

The dilemma facing the Muslim living in an Islamic country is dire. Either accept the implementation of historic Shari'a with its blatant discrimination against women and non-Muslims, and its dependence on the Medina suras; or discard historic Shari'a altogether, and establish a secular state.

It seems that neither of these options would win support.

There is a third possibility.

The sections of historic Shari'a that deal with tolerance and liberty and the question of equality for all human beings – Muslim and non-Muslim – regardless of sex and religion, are based on texts of the Qur'ān and the Sunnah that derive from the Medina period. Mahmoud Taha proposed that following Q2[106] the Medina texts could be set aside as having fulfilled their purpose, and replaced by various texts of the Qur'ān and the Sunnah dealing with the same matters that originated in the Meccan period, and that had been postponed, not abrogated permanently.

Were his suggestion to be acted upon, the positive effects of the changes that would follow would filter through to Muslims living in non-Muslim countries; and grounds for fostering Islamic extremism and religiously motivated violence in Muslim communities would be effectively countered.

Mahmoud Taha's teaching met with fierce hostility from the contemporary orthodox Sudanese Islamic establishment, with Islamic scholars, sectarian leaders and the Muslim Brotherhood calling for the total imposition of historic Shari'a.

He was arrested on Saturday 5 January 1985. His trial, on 7 January lasted two hours. He and four others were sentenced to be hanged. His appeal was rejected. President Numeiri confirmed the verdict and Ustadh Mahmoud Mohamed Taha was hanged on 18 January 1985. His body was taken by helicopter into the desert west of Omdurman, and buried in an unmarked grave.

His courageous and far-seeing spirit lives on, however, in the many Muslims throughout the world who try to spread his message of equality, tolerance, peace and brotherhood. Their number is growing. They refuse to untune the string.

Granted the complexity of the problems and the choices facing the Muslim populations of Islamic countries and of host countries beyond the Dar al-Islam, some readers may think that the task facing the followers of Mahmoud Muhamed Taha is unrealizable.

I am more hopeful, and I think that Jacques Maritain, if I've understood him correctly, would be hopeful as well. He notes,

> Equality of rights is the basic tenet of modern democratic societies. … It should be pointed out that the subjects of rights are not abstract entities like 'truth' or 'error', but human persons taken individually or collectively … the principle of equality of rights is to be applied – not to 'doctrines' or 'creeds', this would have no meaning – but to the citizens who belong in these different religious lineages … who compose the body politic.[12]

The beneficiaries of the principles that the Sudanese imam was promoting, and for which he was hanged in 1985 – equality of rights, justice, tolerance, freedom of speech and movement, peace, brotherhood – are not abstract ideas but 'human beings, taken individually or collectively'. If the human beings concerned really believe in these principles, and have the will to benefit from acceptance of them, then they will have a means to put an end to the cruelty and the chaos that is tearing apart their world and ours, and endangering everybody, including them and their loved ones.

CHAPTER 12

The Afghan Trap

Sowing Seeds of Islamic Extremism

GREEK MYTHOLOGY warned us millennia ago not to open Pandora's Box,[1] and there is an old Arabic proverb (or it may be just a proverb in Arabic), that I'm fond of quoting, about 'not untying the tethered elephant'.[2]

William Shakespeare's *Julius Caesar*[3] has an anguished Mark Antony crying out: 'Cry Havoc! Let slip the dogs of War!' and Shakespeare, in *Henry V*, warns anyone foolish enough to 'let slip' i.e. unleash, these 'dogs of war,' that they have names, and their names were 'famine,' 'sword' and 'fire'.[4] These days, however, they go by the names of 'al-Qaeda,' 'Taliban,' and 'ISIS'.

US and Western Foreign Policy seems adept at untying elephants; and having untied them, at being unable to spot them in the room as they rampage around, wreaking destruction.

Soviet Intervention in Afghanistan

The nine-year military occupation of Afghanistan by Soviet Russian military forces from December 1979 to February 1988, is a case in point.

It was not at all what it appeared to be, any more than were the subsequent US and Western sponsored wars in Iraq, Libya or Syria.

In July 1979 the CIA – not the US military – began to fund and arm Afghan Islamic insurgents, the so-called *mujahidun*, against the pro-Russian government in Kabul headed by Nur Muḥammad Taraki, with the intention of provoking Soviet intervention in Afghanistan.[5]

The very term 'mujahidun' – which means 'Islamic fighters waging a jihad' – should have warned the Carter Administration to exercise prudence and caution before arming and training them, and before accepting the aid of Saudi Arabia, China and Pakistan in doing it.

> The United States supplied funds, weapons and general supervision. Saudi Arabia matched United States financial contributions, and China's government sold and donated weapons. But the dominant operational role on the front lines belonged to Pakistan's ISI (the Inter-services Intelligence Directorate), which insisted on control.[6]

In an interview years later with the French weekly newspaper *Le Nouvel Observateur*,[7] Zbigniew Brzezinski, US

President Carter's National Security Adviser at the time, was asked to confirm that the US had in fact, started to support the Islamist fighters six months before the Soviets invaded, and not in response to that invasion.

Brzezinski admitted that the official version – that the CIA only started helping the insurgents in early 1980 – was false. He added that

> on July 3, [1979] President Carter signed the first directive about clandestine assistance to opponents of the pro-Soviet regime in Kabul. That same day I wrote a note to the President in which I explained to him that, in my opinion, this aid would help bring about military intervention by the Soviets.

When *Le Nouvel Observateur* asked if this wasn't tantamount to 'provoking' the Soviets to intervene, he replied: 'We didn't push the Russians to intervene, but we knowingly increased the probability that they would.'

And they did.

Brzezinski was then asked whether he regretted having 'provoked' the Soviets into intervening. To this he replied:

> What's to regret? That secret operation was an excellent idea. It drew the Russians into the Afghan trap, and you want me to regret it ? ... When the Soviets officially crossed the frontier I wrote to President Carter along these lines,

'We've now got a chance to give the Soviet Union its Vietnam War'.

The Toll of Dead and Wounded

In retrospect, that allegedly 'excellent idea' helped bring about the deaths of over one million Afghans between 1979 and 1988; it led to almost five million refugees fleeing Afghanistan, and two million others being displaced internally. Three million Afghans – mostly civilians – were wounded. 14,500 Russian soldiers died, and 35,000 were wounded. No US military personnel were involved, but behind the scenes, members of the Carter Administration and the CIA were pulling the strings.

Many thousands of the sons of those refugees and the displaced Afghans would eventually come back to haunt the US and their allies,[8] returning to Afghanistan as members of the Taliban, after receiving Islamist tuition and extremism from Deobandi madrasas in Pakistan.

The Deobandis were and still are much influenced by the Wahhabi version of Islam spread worldwide by Petro-dollars from the apparently bottomless pockets of the Saudis. The latter were, as was stated above, matching dollar for dollar the US funding of the Islamic fighters, among whom was Usama bin Laden, self-confessed mastermind of the horrors of 9/11.[9]

Andrew Hartman, in a paper that described graphically the cold calculus of US decision makers, points out that Afghanistan remained a country of relative unimportance to the USA, or so it seemed; and yet the US decision to finance and arm the most fundamentalist and dangerous Muslim fighters that could be rounded up, is a decision that continues to shake the world:

> This blatant disregard for the people of Afghanistan is nothing new. For basic security purposes – beyond the morality issue that US leaders will not stoop to discuss unless it supports their policy – this disregard has always been a big mistake. The mujihadin [*sic*] of the 1980s may have been cannon fodder for US interests, but ... Afghanistan became a launching pad for jihad worldwide, and the USA, with its overreaching geopolitical goals, became the target. Too much attention to money, trade and oil, and not enough attention to the capabilities of a well-trained and well-armed fanatical religious group, made for bad policy. None of us is the safer for the US role in Soviet-occupied Afghanistan.[10]

Over the years the numbers of radicalized foreigners involved in some way with the mujahidun in Afghanistan is estimated to have grown to more than 100,000.[11] Many of these were to fight in Iraq, and Libya, and more recently, in Syria. This was predicted.

> Into the political vacuum left by 20 years of war and the collapse of stable government, has marched a new generation of violent fundamentalists, nurtured and inspired by the Taliban's unique Islamist model. Thousands

> of foreign extremists now fighting alongside the Taliban in Afghanistan are determined to, someday, overthrow their own regimes and carry out Taliban-style Islamist revolutions in their homelands.[12]

In the light of the tragic consequences of 9/11, and granted the ongoing lamentable record of US, UK, Australian and allied involvement in a country riven by bloody civil war, an endless supply of arms, and export of drugs, one can only regret that the CIA didn't more thoroughly consider the long-term consequences of provoking a Soviet intervention in Afghanistan, before they started funding and arming local and foreign *mujahidun* to harass the Communist government there.

The Soviets seem to have read the signs of the times better than the US. The fall of the Shah on 16 January 1979 and the return of the Ayatollah Khomeini from exile in Paris to power in Iran on 1 February 1979, along with extremist jihadi groups appearing in Afghanistan, boded ill for security in the central Asiatic republics of the then-USSR. The Russians were reluctant to allow Afghanistan to fall to Islamist extremists because of the probable long-term consequences for the region. Their fears were justified.

By covertly aiding the Islamic insurgents, it was the Americans who fell into what Brzezinski so aptly called 'the Afghan trap.'

Over its almost 10 years duration, that war is estimated to have cost the USSR $96 billion. The US, on the other hand, spent little more than $2 billion, without a single US soldier putting a foot in the country. Up till then.

But it had sown seeds of hate that will take decades to eradicate.

It would be sad beyond words if there were to be some truth in what sociologist Claudio Véliz said of certain members of the US intelligentsia – that they are 'generally far happier when hated than when ignored'.[13]

Some analysts, like Thomas Friedman, assure us that 'the super-empowered angry men [terrorists] have no specific ideological program or demands. Rather they are driven by a generalized hatred of the US, Israel and other supposed enemies of Islam.'[14]

Usama bin Laden, killed by US Navy SEALS on 1 May 2011, disagreed. He wrote to the American allies on 12 November 2002: 'Just as you kill, so you shall be killed; just as you bomb, so you shall be bombed. And there will be more to come.'[15] An independently published list of Bin Laden's grievances, highly itemised – not at all generalized – goes for 275 pages.[16]

What happened in Afghanistan from 1979 to 1988 is reminiscent of Churchill's aiding the Communists in Yugoslavia during WWII despite the inevitability of a Communist government in Yugoslavia after the war.

Without any monitoring by the CIA most of the US weapons were given to *mujahidun* who were openly dedicated to setting up an Islamic and anti-American regime in Kabul when the Russians left.

And after the Russians left, the US weapons for the mujahidun kept coming.[17]

> The camps in Pakistan and Afghanistan where they [the *mujahidun*] trained became virtual universities for promoting pan-Islamic extremism in Algeria, Egypt, Yemen, Sudan, Jordan, Indonesia, Malaysia, the Philippines, and Bangladesh. Americans woke up to the danger only in 1993, when Afghan-trained Arab militants blew up the World Trade Center in New York, killing six people and injuring 1,000. The bombers believed that, just as Afghanistan had defeated one superpower – the Soviet Union – they would defeat a second.[18]

Readers may well wonder what might have happened in Afghanistan if the US had not intervened by arming and training the *mujahidun*, and especially by drawing the Soviets into the conflict. Would the Russians have turned the tables on the US, defeated the jihadists and been the first foreign power in centuries to control the country through their surrogates in Kabul?

Some Americans analysts did seem surprised in 1980 to discover that having enticed the Soviets into their trap, they may have put a potentially victorious Moscow within striking distance of the Persian Gulf, with the possibility of a straight run through Afghanistan to the Indian Ocean, and the Asian sub-continent.[19]

'There Is No Global Islamism'

What would have happened if Carter had won the Presidential election in 1980? The indications are that like Reagan, Carter would have ensured that the *mujahidun* were well-trained and well-armed – oblivious of the Islamic fighters' long-term goal of fighting the US and their allies after they had driven the Russians out of the country.[20]

During his interview with *Le Nouvel Observateur* Brzezinski was asked:

> Don't you regret having favoured Islamic fundamentalists; and having given weapons and training to future terrorists?

Brzezinski replied:

> What's more important with regard to world history: a few excitable Islamists or the liberation of Central Europe and the end of the Cold War? … it is said that the West should have a Global Politic with regard to global Islamism. This is foolish. There is no global Islamism.[21]

***

There have been almost 2,400 US military deaths in Afghanistan since 2001 when the US invaded, in the wake of 9/11. 20,049 military personnel have been wounded in action. President Trump authorised an additional 4,000 US forces to Afghanistan in 2017.[22] This is the longest war in US history. About 11% of the adult homeless population in the USA are military veterans.[23]

Forty-one Australian soldiers have been killed and 261 wounded in Afghanistan, the majority since October 2007. We were unable to obtain a figure for the percentage of military veterans among our homeless adults, but many of them suffer from homelessness, family break-up, inability to find work and post-traumatic stress disorder (PTSD). From 2001 to 2014, 291 defence force personnel committed suicide; and between 2011 and November 2015, 95 Australian veterans committed suicide according to the latest figures available.[24]

CHAPTER 13

Iraq and Syria

Lessons to Be Learned

WRITING IN the late 1840s, George Grote, author of a 12-volume history of Ancient Greece up to the time of Alexander the Great, despaired of being able 'to enumerate the multiplied and irreconcilable discrepancies in regard to every step' of an old genealogy of the rulers and heroes of the city of Argos in the Peleponnesus.[1]

Imagine the despair of Grote if he were to be given the task of reconciling the myriad and irreconcilable discrepancies confronting anyone trying to make sense of media comment and political spin on the Invasion of Iraq, and the so-called civil war in Syria, and their catastrophic impact on the region and our world.

Grote was trying to separate myth and poetic licence from history. 21st century readers who care about what is happening in the world must wrestle with the task of separating truth from lies, reality from propaganda and prejudice, and facts from the omnipresent seductive fantasies.

Pyrrhic Victory

In the aftermath of the horror of 9/11, the US invasion of Iraq code-named *Iraqi Freedom* was authorised by Congress in October 2002, and launched on 20 March 2003.

Militarily speaking, the invasion was a success for the US and their allies, including Australia. But it was a Pyrrhic victory that came at a terrible cost to all concerned. Where the Americans fell down was in the post-invasion occupation, because they had no realistic plan for post Saddam Hussein Iraq. In fact, they had no vision of the end state that they wanted. It was that lack of vision that inexorably led to brutal and guerrilla warfare on the part of insurgents armed to the teeth with weapons that should never have fallen into their hands.

Ignorance of Islam and its history, coupled with the usual western illusions about replacing dictatorship with 'democracy,' and arrogance in underestimating the strength of religious culture and traditions, also played their part.

The US and their allies found themselves bogged down in a quagmire of violence, until they withdrew in December 2011.

The invasion of Iraq officially 'ended' on 1 May 2003 but the ill-planned occupation was to drag on for more than another eight years, and to be accompanied by myriad deaths on all sides, and country-wide destruction.

The much spun pretext for the massive military intervention was Saddam Hussein's alleged stockpiles of weapons of mass destruction (WMD). Its goal was, of course, regime change in Iraq: the removal of Saddam Hussein from power.

Mission Accomplished

Rebuilding the country after the liberated Iraqis held free elections and voted in a democratic government, was to be in the capable hands of selected US companies. That, at least, was the theory.

The Guardian reported that, 'a subsidiary of Halliburton, the firm formerly headed by the US vice-president, Dick Cheney,' was a member of 'one of four consortia whose bids were invited in a secret process,' in April 2003.

Several of the firms were, again according to *The Guardian*, major Republican Party donors.[2]

Six weeks later to the day, on 1 May 2003, President George W. Bush, landed in a navy jet fighter on the USS *Abraham Lincoln* off the coast of California. While a banner declaring 'Mission Accomplished' waved above him he announced 'Major combat operations in Iraq have ended. In the battle of Iraq, the United States and our allies have prevailed.'[3]

All may have seemed done and dusted to the politicians, analysts and military tacticians who planned the invasion and were safely out of harm's way in Washington, but 'tinkering with regime change,' whether it be in Iraq, Egypt, Libya or Syria, 'has proven itself to be the most dangerous of games.'[4]

As a direct result of the decision to invade Iraq, there were horrific and ongoing consequences for Iraq, for all its people, for the invading and occupying forces, for the whole of the region and for the US and the world.

Fourteen years of intermittent and bloody sectarian conflict between Sunni and Shia, and between US troops and insurgents and numerous varieties of al-Qa'eda including the nemesis of all, the self-styled 'Islamic State,' wreaked a terrible toll in human lives, mindless violence and destruction of property and infrastructure.

Fake News

Some time after 1 May, George W. Bush agreed that 'putting 'mission accomplished' on an aircraft carrier was a mistake,' but as far as I know he has not yet admitted that intervening in Iraq on a trumped up pretext, was a deplorable error of judgement.[5]

Speaking of 'trumped up pretexts,' on 6 April 2017 neophyte US President Donald Trump learned of an attack with chemical weapons on the rebel-held city of Khan Sheikhoun, in war-ravaged Syria.

Without producing any cogent evidence, and assuming that Syrian President Bashar al-Assad had ordered the attack, President Trump ordered US forces to strike at the Syrian Air Force Base in Shayrat near Homs.

Fifty-nine Tomahawk missiles were launched from warships in the eastern Mediterranean. According to the Americans all missiles hit their target. The Russians say that only twenty-three hit the base.

President Trump called on 'all civilized nations to join us in seeking to end the slaughter and bloodshed in Syria, and also to end terrorism of all kinds and all types.'[6]

No one could quarrel with the President's call for ending the bloodshed in Syria. But his missile attack – not authorised by Congress – allegedly killed six people on the base, and nine others in surrounding villages. These latter appear to have been killed by the missiles that overshot the base.[7]

This is not the first time that Bashar al-Assad has been gratuitously accused of engaging in chemical warfare.

In August 2013, *Médicins sans Frontières* reported that at least 355 people in Damascus and Ghouta, a suburb of Damascus, had died from what appeared to be a neuro-toxic agent.[8]

Like President Trump on 6 April 2017, the US and others also rushed to judgement almost four years earlier, in August 2013.

The then-Secretary of State John Kerry accused the Syrian government of a cover-up in 'a cowardly crime' and a 'moral obscenity' that shocked the world's conscience. He claimed that the Obama administration had 'undeniable' evidence 'that the Assad government was culpable in the use of chemical weapons on civilians' in the 21 August attack in Damascus suburbs.[9]

Reports that the Administration of Democratic President Barak Obama was considering a military strike against the Assad government continued to circulate. The then-citizen Donald Trump even tweeted President Obama twice, warning him that no good would come of attacking Syria.[10]

Meanwhile, UN weapon inspectors in Syria were fired upon by snipers as they attempted to investigate the site of the 21 August attack.[11]

Who Benefits?

Bashar al-Assad rejected charges that his government forces used chemical weapons, describing the claims as 'preposterous' and 'completely politicized,' as the *Los Angeles Times* reported.[12]

And *The Times* went on to quote the head of Russia's Parliamentary International Affairs Committee, Aleksey Pushkov, on his Twitter account, according to *BBC Monitoring*, which translates foreign media reports:

> The West does not want to answer the main question: Why would Assad use chemical weapons? To give grounds for invasion? To dig his own grave?[13]

UN investigator Carla Del Ponte said that there was strong evidence that the rebels used chemical weapons; but there was no evidence linking the Syrian government to the use of such weapons. But she added that more investigation was needed.

Del Ponte was no stranger to the world of spin, prejudice and political rumour-mongering. In 1999 she had been appointed to head the UN war crimes tribunals for Yugoslavia and Rwanda, and she continued as the chief prosecutor for the Yugoslav tribunal until 2008.[14]

Bashar al-Assad never denied that Syria had chemical weapons. In 2013 he denied that Syria had used them against the rebels and civilians. When pressed he agreed to the Chemical Weapons Convention with the UN, on 12 September 2013, and by 23 June 2014 all declared chemicals in Syria had been removed by the UN inspectors.

The US army destroyed 600 metric tons of Syria's stockpile in just six weeks.[15]

The Syrian President continues to be vilified and accused of the 'chemical weapons attack' on 4 April 2017, on Syrian civilians in a rebel-held town in southern Idlib province, viz. Khan Sheikhoun.

Assumptions of Assad's 'certain' guilt continue to be offered without proof by the media, and accepted as 'fact' globally by over-trusting heirs to the 'information revolution'.

Presumption of Guilt

A group of top former US military and Intelligence officials – all named in the source available to us and noted below – was formed in 2003 when they became aware that their former colleagues had been ordered to manufacture intelligence to 'justify' a war with Iraq.

They have spoken against the US's presuming without evidence that Assad was guilty of using chemical weapons in the attack against Khan Shaikhoun on 4 April:

> Our US Army contacts in the area have told us this is not what happened. There was no Syrian 'chemical weapons attack'. Instead, a Syrian aircraft bombed an al-Qaeda ammunition depot that turned out to be full of noxious chemicals and a strong wind blew the chemical-laden cloud over a nearby village where many consequently died.

Assad has publicly denied any involvement in the deaths, and said that not only did he not have any chemical weapons, but he would not use them if he had them.

The group of former Intelligence and military officials went on:

The mandate of the UN's Organization for the Prohibition of Chemical Weapons was to ensure that all were destroyed – like the mandate for the UN inspectors for Iraq regarding WMD. The UN inspectors' findings on WMD were the truth. Rumsfeld and his generals lied and this seems to be happening again. The stakes are even higher now; the importance of a relationship of trust with Russia's leaders cannot be overstated.

We issued our first Memorandum for the President on the afternoon of Feb. 5, 2003. Addressing President Bush, we closed with these words: 'No one has a corner on the truth; nor do we harbour illusions that our analysis is "irrefutable" or "undeniable" (adjectives Secretary of State Colin Powell applied to his charges against Saddam Hussein). But after watching Secretary Powell today, we are convinced that you would be well served if you widened the discussion … beyond the circle of those advisers clearly bent on a war for which we see no compelling reason and from which we believe the unintended consequences are likely to be catastrophic.' Respectfully, we offer the same advice to you, President Trump.[16]

CHAPTER 14

Political Islam

Reflections

IN THESE days of extremist, political Islam, attempts by non-Muslims, or even by Muslims, to discuss or study critically the nature and history of Islam and its sacred and religious literature, are often represented as attacks on Islam or on Muslims.

This is especially true of attempts to discuss or study the text of the Qur'ān. Since the beginning of the 9th century Muslims have been forbidden to interpret the text. The so-called 'door of interpretation' the *'bāb al-Ijtihād'* remains closed for Sunni Muslims to this day.[1] Even attempting to understand the Qur'ān could be seen as a wish to challenge it.[2]

For centuries this decision has posed a serious problem for Sunni Islam, the majority sect of Islam. Since interpreting the Qur'ān is forbidden, modern-day Muslims wanting to distance themselves from suicide bombers and extremists, and from an inflexible politico-religious system that is becoming embedded in its 7th century Bedouin culture and origins, find themselves isolated and reduced to silence.

Extremist Wahhabists and Salafists, on the other hand, control many of the world's mosques and subscribe to the view of Sheikh Yūsuf al-Qaradāwī, religious guide of the Muslim Brothers, that killing people who leave Islam is essential: 'An apostate is to be killed'.[3]

Following the terrorist attack by 22-year-old Salman Ramadan Abedi,[4] that killed 22 – mainly young girls and their mothers – and wounded 59, as they attended a concert by American singer Ariana Grande in Manchester on 22 May 2017,[5] a brief debate took place on Sydney TV Channel 7 Sunrise programme between a controversial Shi'ite Imam Mohammed Tawhidi, and a prominent Sunni community leader Dr Jamal Rifi.[6]

The subject: the causes of extremism of young Muslims in Australia and around the world.

The imam produced an Al-Qaeda flag that he said he purchased from a Melbourne shop, and went on,

> These things can be obtained from anywhere, even online or on the Internet, but when you have stores openly selling these items … creating this Jihadi atmosphere for the youth to put on their cars … Our books teach the beheading of people … The Islamic scriptures are exactly what is pushing these people to behead the infidel … the person who killed the young girls in Manchester did so believing he was going to dine with the prophet Muhammed that very night.

In his reply, Dr Rifi, who roundly condemned the Manchester bombing in his opening remarks, said:

> I don't know where the Imam's got his information from. The [Islamic] Scriptures existed for hundreds of years, they did not incite violence or terror acts; it is an ideology of the so-called Islamic State and they are actually targeting the vulnerable young people ... there is nothing in our religion that would support the killing of innocent people.

At this point the discussion degenerated into a cacophany, with each speaking loudly over the other, and ended abruptly.

Whatever may be the truth behind harsh criticisms of the young Imam and questions about his religious status,[7] fair-minded people reading the Islamic Holy Books and other respected literature would know that the Imam had good reasons for being concerned, and that whatever modern polemicists may claim, the Qur'ān and the sunna (Islamic traditions connected to Muḥammad) emerged at a time of great economic hardship and social unrest and cruelty, and have given rise to acts of violence and oppression.

Anyone doubting this should read Ibn Ishāq's *Life of Muhammad*, or Al-Bukhārī or Al-Tirmidhī or another of the authors of the six recognized collections of Hadith, or Al-Tabarī's *History of the Prophets and Kings*, or *The Conquest of Abyssinia* by Shihāb ad-Dīn Ahmad ibn 'Abd al-Qāder, or myriad other works, in addition to the Qur'ān.

Ibn Ishāq's biography of Muḥammad, written in the eighth century, was preceded by a number of earlier biographies that were called *Kitāb al-Maghāzī, The Book of the Military Campaigns.* These took their name from the 80 or so military campaigns and raids (*ghazawāt*), conducted by Muḥammad during his ten years in Medina. According to Ibn Ishāq, Muḥammad participated in 19 of these raids and pillaging expeditions. In the words of Egyptian Jesuit priest Samir Khalil Samir, a well-known Arabist and leading commentator on Islamic literature and culture,

> Violence was definitely a part of the rapid rise and expansion of Islam. At the time, no one found anything blameworthy in Muhammad's military actions since wars were part of the Arab Bedouin culture. Today, the problem is that the fiercest Muslim groups keep adopting that model. They say, 'We have to take Islam to non-Muslims as the Prophet did, through war and violence,' and they base these statements on some verses from the Qur'ān.[8]

And not just the Qur'ān. Reinhart Dozy, the pre-eminent authority on Spanish Islam, notes that,

> In the ninth century the Christians in many cities including Cordova, were ruined or impoverished. In other words, that happened in Spain which happened in every other country conquered by the Arabs; their rule, at first mild and humane, degenerated into intolerable despotism. From

> the ninth century onwards, the conquerors of the Peninsular followed to the letter the Khalif 'Omar's blunt advice: 'We must devour the Christians; and our descendants must devour theirs so long as Islam endures'.[9]

The day after the inconclusive debate described above took place, 28 Coptic Christians were gunned down on a bus travelling to a monastery near the city of Minya in Egypt. The attack was launched by masked terrorists who arrived in three pick-up trucks and opened fire on the passengers, many of whom were children. Egyptian intelligence believes the Minya attack was led by ISIS jihadists based in Libya.[10]

Five days later, more than 80 people, mainly civilians on their way to work in Kabul, were brutally murdered and 460 injured, in a massive vehicle bombing in Afghanistan;[11] and a young Australian Muslim girl and 14 others were murdered in Baghdad by ISIS, which boasted that it was targeting Shiite Muslims in the suicide bombing – even though the bombing occurred in a Christian quarter.[12]

Eight days later, on June 3, three suicide bombers killed 12 people and wounded 90, while mourners were attending a funeral in Kabul.

Father Samir Khalil Samir, whom we quoted above, noted some years ago, that

> Today the problem is that, whatever their position, Muslims will not admit that some verses of the Qur'ān no longer have relevance for present situations. Therefore, the 'ulemā'

> (Qur'anic doctors of the law) are obliged to say that they do not agree with those who choose to adopt the Verse of the Sword as normative, even if they cannot condemn them. Consequently, in the Qur'ān there are two different choices, the aggressive and the peaceful, and both of them are acceptable. There is a need for an authority, unanimously acknowledged by Muslims, that could say: From now on, only this verse is valid. But this does not – and probably will never – happen. This means that when some fanatics kill children, women, and men in the name of pure and authentic Islam, or in the name of the Qur'ān or of the Muslim tradition, nobody can tell them: 'You are not true and authentic Muslims.' All they can say is: 'Your reading of Islam is not ours.' And this is the ambiguity of Islam, from its beginning to the present day: violence is a part of it, although it is also possible to choose tolerance; tolerance is a part of it, but it is also possible to choose violence.[13]

It is not uncommon when questions about the rights and position of women in Islam arise, to find the media quoting young and articulate Muslim women who emphatically deny that Islam poses any threat to the well-being and happiness of women.

The implication appears to be that Sunni Islam, the sect to which most Muslims in Australia belong, must be moderate and peaceful, and the Islamic Holy Books can't contain anything likely to radicalize young Muslims, because these Muslim girls are articulate and content with their lot.

Readers may recall that in 2011 the Australian Federation of Islamic Councils argued that Islamic Law, Sharia, 'guarantees women's rights that are not recognised in mainstream Australian courts.'[14]

This claim about 'women's rights' has to be seen in the light of the following:

> # The Australian Federal Police investigated 69 incidents of forced or under-age marriage in the 2015–2016 financial year, up from 33 the previous year.
>
> # There are no official figures but it is estimated that there are 83,000 women and girls in Australia who may have been subjected to female genital mutilation.
>
> # The Royal Commission into Institutional Responses to Child Sexual Abuse, which has spent the past four years probing numerous religious organizations, has made no inquiries into Islam.[15]

A young Muslim woman, Yassmin Abdel-Magied, recently said on the ABC programme *Q&A*, that Islam was the 'most feminist religion.'[16] It may be instructive to see whether Muslim scholars of the Qur'ān – authors of the better-known tafāsir or 'commentaries' – agree with her on the controversial topic of the place and treatment of women in Islam.

Of the three classic commentators on the Qur'ān – Al-Tabari (died 923), al-Zamakhshari (died 1143) and al-Baidawi (died 1286) – the latter, 'Abdullah bin 'Umar al-Baidawi is the most popular and respected authority, and reputedly the most quoted, despite his acknowledged lack of originality.

Commenting on Sura 12 of the Qur'ān and on the expression referring there to Jacob, 'think of me as in my dotage,' in verse 94, al-Baidawi notes that *dotage* [مفند = خرف]

> is deficiency of intellect arising from old age. Consequently one does not talk about an 'old woman in her dotage' because deficiency of intellect is an essential characteristic of a woman.[17]

Lest it should be thought that Baidawi was expressing some personal, misogynistic, view at variance with traditional Islamic thought, Abu al-Qasim Mahmud ibn 'Umar al-Zamakhshari (died 1143) comments:

> A woman, even when young, is not endowed with wits, so her wits cannot be said to fail in old age.[18]

Edward William Lane, in his Lexicon,[19] cites seven authorities who concur that 'unsound of mind because of extreme old age [مفند]' cannot be used of a woman 'because she has not possessed judgement [even] in her youth'. One source added, 'at any time'.[20]

The study of these tafāsir, or commentaries, and therefore of the writings of Baidawi and Zamakhshiri among others, is an essential part of the education in Islamic madrasas. Along with the hadith (sayings of Muḥammad) and fikh (Islamic principles of jurisprudence) the tafāsir feature as elements in traditional Islamic curricula.[21]

As well as featuring young Muslim women who may or may not be free in what they say, the media might also interview young Muslim men, and ask them if they agree with the views of Baidawi and Zamakhshari in regard to women; and if they agree with sayings attributed to Muḥammad found in various hadith that deal with the same subject.

For instance, al-Bukhārī records in his collection of hadith, that Abu Said Al-Khudri related how

> once when Allah's apostle [Muḥammad] went out ... he passed by some women and said 'O women! Give alms, as I have seen that the majority of the dwellers in Hell-fire were you (women).' They asked, 'Why is it so, O Allah's apostle?' He replied, 'You curse frequently, and are ungrateful to your husbands. I have not seen anyone more deficient in intelligence and religion than you. A cautious sensible man could be led astray by some of you'. The women asked, 'O Allah's apostle! What is deficient in our intelligence and religion?' He said, 'Is not the evidence of two women equal to the witness of one man?' They replied in the affirmative. He said, 'This is the deficiency in your intelligence. Isn't it true that a woman can neither pray nor fast during her menses?' The women replied in the affirmative. He said: 'This is the deficiency in your religion.'[22]

As for the view of woman generally reflected in the Qur'ān, the recently published *Encyclopaedia of the Qur'ān* sums up the concept of woman found in it as follows:

> undoubtedly [it is] that of a being who is considered to be weak, flawed or passive ... not surprisingly, the earth is female and humans consider themselves her masters … Women's subaltern status is reflected in verses that position them among orphans, children, and men who are too weak to fight.[23]

These are matters of some moment. Especially when most Muslims consider the Qur'ān to be the words of God, not the words of Muḥammad.

The media have their own agenda for giving air time to attractive young Muslim women whose opinions often ignore or contradict the interpretation of the Qur'ān given above. But if politicians and the media are genuinely interested in the truth, let them also canvass the views of the brothers, fathers and husbands of these young women.

We think that most Muslims came to Australia seeking a new and happier life than the one they had in their homeland. All who are genuinely interested in putting an end to extremism of young Australian Muslims, and improving the lot of Muslim women in Australia, should encourage well-informed and courageous Muslims from all our Islamic communities – Sunni, Shia, Ismaili, Ahmadi, Alevi, Sufi, Alawite, Ibadi and Druze among others – to express their views fearlessly on how best to achieve this.

CHAPTER 15

Joining The Dots

Zero Tolerance for Extremist Islam

AUSTRALIAN Prime Minister Scott Morrison has gone on record as saying that 'Islamist extremism … present[s] the most dangerous form of radicalism in Australia.'[1]

He was speaking in the wake of Melbourne's Bourke Street terrorist attack on Saturday 10 November 2018 in which Italian restaurateur Mr Sisto Malaspina was stabbed to death, and two other bystanders as well as police officers were wounded. The Somali-born perpetrator, identified as Hassan Khalif Shire Ali, allegedly came under the influence of ISIS and has been identified by the so-called 'Islamic State' group, as one of its members.

Mr Morrison went on to say that the greatest threat of religious extremism 'is the radical and dangerous ideology of extremist Islam.'

He praised Muslim Australians who were trying to protect their children from radicalisation, and commended 'these

Australians for the leadership and courage that I know they have had to show … often at great risk to themselves and their families.'[2]

Reaction from some sections of the Muslim community to the response of the PM to the Bourke Street attack was quick. It ranged from the PM's comments being 'ignorant,' 'politically desperate,'[3] 'racist and simplistic,' and 'scapegoating' the Muslim community,[4] to 'divisive,' 'politicising the incident,' and 'using it for political gain.'[5]

Australia's Grand Mufti Ibrahim Abu Mohamed 'rejected government calls for Muslim community leaders to do more to combat radicalism,'[6] and said that the PM's comments 'constituted "serious discrimination" against Australia's Muslim community".'[7]

Labor MP Anne Aly said that Mr Morrison needed to do 'a little bit of terrorism 101 … and know what he's talking about before he starts dividing communities and pointing fingers at extremist Islam.'[8]

Yet extremist Sunni Islam, the political face of Islam, is the proverbial 'elephant in the room'; and it is extremist Islam, not the PM, that is dividing the community.

The few thoughts that follow are inspired and encouraged by a courageous Sudanese Imam, Mahmoud Muḥammad Taha, who foresaw the situation faced today by Sunni Muslim communities and their democratic host countries.

The imam's efforts to prevent what is today called 'extremism,' and to forestall the rise of extremist Islamic sects like Al-Shabaab, Boko Haram, the Deobandists[9] and the Taliban, Jemaah Islamiyah, ISIS, and al-Qaeda and their

Salafist and Wahhabist ilk, led to his being executed at the age of 76 as a heretic, by a decision handed down in a mock trial ordered by Sudanese President Nimeiry, on January 18, 1985.[10]

Differences

The welcome given to Islamic refugees, and governmental funding of ways to help them integrate into Western democracies, contrast sharply with the wretched conditions under which many non-Muslims or other Muslim minorities, live in countries dominated by Sunni Islamic culture and law – the same Law that many would wish to introduce into Western Societies.

In many Islamic countries non-Muslims and a-political Muslims have to keep their 'differences' below the radar in order to go about their lives in peace. Non-Muslim women may be obliged to wear the hijab or burqa if they wish to go out in public. Non-Muslims may be forbidden to practise their religion publicly, to bring into the Islamic country prayer books, missals or bibles or even rosary beads, and crucifixes, and are not allowed to buy or to drink alcohol, or eat pork.

In most Western democracies, on the other hand, Muslims have been treated with consideration and respect, often, nevertheless, provoking claims similar to the ones expressed in the aftermath of the Bourke Street attack, that 'Muslims' are victims of discrimination because of their religion: that they are being 'scapegoated' because they are different in their dress, religious and social laws and customs.

Two assumptions seem to underlie much media coverage of Muslims in non-Islamic societies: that they are, in fact, discriminated against because they are different; and that Islamic societies based on the Qur'ān and Islamic Law, respect differences.

Many of the 'differences' in dress and religions and social customs between Muslims and non-Muslims would have been unfamiliar to the average citizen of all Western democratic host-countries when first encountered.

As unfamiliar as were, years ago, the turbans and beards that Sikh men wear, or the traditional saris of Indian women, or the yarmulke or skullcap worn by some Jewish men, or the facial and other tattoos of Maoris and some other Pacific Islanders, or the habits worn by Catholic nuns.

Yet, to the best of my knowledge, none of these differences between Sikhs, Indians, Jews, Maoris, Pacific Islanders, or Catholics, and their fellow Australians, prevented or prevents their integration into Australian society, or their being welcomed and accepted as citizens, ready to obey Australia's laws, and respect our democratic way of life.

Not Compatible

The 'X-factor' that Western politicians and media – in thrall to political correctness – seem unable or unwilling to confront, is extremist Sunni political Islam and its Law.

Far from respecting 'differences,' these latter fear and shun them, and brook no opposition or criticism. Critics are subjected either to character assassination, or to physical intimidation and death. The recent alleged torture and gruesome murder of Saudi journalist Jamal Khashoggi is a case in point.[11]

And not just critics – also members of vulnerable minorities like Asia Bibi, a poor Catholic wife and mother, in heavily radicalized Muslim Pakistan.

Asia Bibi's release from gaol after the Supreme Court overturned her 2010 sentencing to death for alleged blasphemy, was delayed, 'after authorities agreed to prevent her from flying abroad following talks with extremist Sunni Islamists who want her publicly hanged.'[12]

The agreement between the government and the Tehreek-e-Labbaik party was reached in the city of Lahore, where Islamists had been rallying for days.

Bibi's acquittal has posed a challenge to the government of Pakistan's new prime minister, the former cricketer Imran Khan, who came to power recently 'partly by pursuing the Islamist agenda.'[13]

Frequently, the fate of Islamic minorities like Shi'a, Ismailis, Druze, Alawites Sufis, Alevis, Zaidis and Ahmadis, is murderous violence[14] or imprisonment at the hands of their fellow Muslims in many Islamic countries, among them Saudi Arabia, Pakistan, Turkey, Syria and Yemen,[15] and Malaysia.[16]

Zaidis, a sect of the Shi'a, represent about 35% of the Muslim population of Yemen, with Sunnis 65%. Houthi rebels who comprise a mix of Zaidi and Sunni, appear to be involved in a political, rather than a sectarian, conflict.

No one should doubt, however, that differences *do* matter to extremist political Islamists, especially to Al-Qaeda in the Arabian Peninsular (AQAP) and to ISIS, both of which have joined Saudi Arabia in attacking Zaidis and Sulaimani and Dawoodi Ismailis in Yemen.

And the few Jews remaining in Yemen share the fate of all the minorities and face, like them, an uncertain future.[17]

Points of convergence between extremist Sunni Islam and despotic totalitarian systems can only be ignored if logic and history are set aside. Tales of families compelled to live under ISIS in Syria and Iraq give the lie to recent claims that Wahhabism or Salafism or Deobandism can be compatible with civilized living in a free, democratic society.

Despite claims to the contrary, many of the Islamic practices that are said to be part of Islamic religious tradition do not take their origin from the Qur'ān.

The word 'hijab,' for instance, occurs seven times in the Qur'ān: Q7^{46}, 33^{53}, 38^{32}, 41^{5}, 42^{51}, 17^{45}, 19^{17}. On none of those occasions does it mean a head covering for women.[18]

Such practices may well be part of the cultural life of an individual Muslim, but they are not all religious or Islamic in origin. Many are derived from the traditions and customs of cultures conquered and assimiliated by Islamist armies in the past; some may be derived from hadith or alleged sayings of Muḥammad.

Depite this uncertainty, Mullah Rafiullah, head of the religious police of the Taliban in Afghanistan, once had 225 women whipped in a single day for violations of the dress code.[19] They were fortunate not to have been killed.

Tolerance or Indifference

The custom some have of wearing the burqa (covering the body and entire face), niqab (covering the body and the face but revealing the eyes) and hijab (covering the hair and back of the head), is also a matter of dispute among many Muslims in Western host-countries, and in some Islamic countries.[20]

It took almost 10 years for the Danish parliament to move on banning the burqa and the niqab or full-face veil. The first attempt to get the parliament to ban them was in 2009. On 31 May 2018, by 75 votes to 30, the Danish parliament finally banned Islamic full-face veils in public. From 1 August 2018 wearing a burqa or a niqab has been an offence.

Denmark follows France, Belgium, the Netherlands, Bulgaria, Austria, Tajikistan, Cameroun, Chad, Republic of Congo, Gabon, Latvia and China.

In 2016, in the New South Wales District Court, Judge Audrey Balla ruled against a Muslim woman's wearing the niqab while giving evidence. There has been no ruling on the wearing of the burqa or the hijab by the Australian Parliament.

John J. Mearsheimer, in his *The Great Delusion: Liberal Dreams and International Realities,* describes a post-Cold War America dedicated to 'regime change' in many Middle Eastern countries, and to turning them into so-called 'liberal democracies,' engineered by US policy makers who, he says, 'know little' about the countries concerned, 'or even the difference between Sunni and Shi'a Islam'. For 'post-Cold War America,' read 'Australia'.

Summing up, Mearsheimer notes that Washington, under Presidents George W. Bush and Barack Obama, played a key role in 'bringing widespread killing and devastation' throughout the Middle East and beyond.

The secular West is not religionless, but it has too many policy-makers and political parties that behave as if it were.

These latter, like their Muslim counterparts, also claim to accept and even welcome 'differences'. They do this in the name of Affirmative Action, Equal Opportunity, Feminism, Multiculturalism, Ethnic Pride, Marriage Equality and myriad politically correct special interest groups; or just plain pragmatism because they need votes.

The West's much vaunted tolerance of 'difference' is often, in reality, a product of thinly disguised indifference, born of incomprehension regarding the present, and ignorance of the past, all shaken up and served with an unhealthy admixture of confusion and an underlying fear – not hatred – of Extremist Islam.

A fear that most non-radicalized Muslims, and most common-sensed non-Muslims who have managed to join some of the dots, would share.

A fear that Mahmoud Muḥammad Taha may well have allayed, had he not been brutally killed by the extremism he strove to eliminate from Islam.

A former radicalized young British Muslim, Ed Husain, who founded the world's first anti-extremism think tank, *Quilliam* in 2008, has advice for all concerned about extremist political Islam and terrorism:

> We cannot reverse the rising tide of jihadism unless we uproot its theology and ideology … As long as the House of Islam provides shelter for Salafi jihadis the rest of the world will attack Islam and Muslims … As long as Muslims tolerate their presence, we will give licence even to the ideologues in both the East and West to conflate Islam with

Salafi-jihadism. More Muslims will turn to jihadism, and another generation will be lost. We need to cleanse our mosques, publishing houses, schools, websites, satellite TV stations, madrases and ministries of Salafi-jihadi influences. Unless we do, Islamophobia will continue to rise, and we cannot complain when the West repeatedly suggests that Muslims are suspect. Unless we do, no matter how much Muslims protest, they will continue to share the opprobrium heaped on those who claim to represent us. Unless we do, we cannot credibly claim that 'they have nothing to do with us'. Sadly, they do come from within us.[21]

Notes

Chapter 1

1 'Qur'ān' has become the accepted English transliteration of the Arabic word for the Muslim Holy Book. It more accurately represents the Arabic than 'Koran,' which formerly was used.

2 Philip K. Hitti, *History of the Arabs,* London, Macmillan, 1968, p. 91.

3 Ibid., *horror vacui*, i.e. 'dread of empty space,' here used figuratively.

4 *Jāhilīyya* occurs four times in the Qur'ān: Q3^{153}, 5^{50}, 33^{33}, and 48^{26}.

5 D.S. Margoliouth, 'God, Arabian, pre-Islamic,' *Encyclopaedia of Religion and Ethics*, ed. James Hastings, Edinburgh, T & T Clarke, 1913, vol. vi, p. 247.

6 The Taghlibi opposed Islam and clung to their Christian faith for a long time. See *The History of al-Tabari*, Albany, State University of New York Press, 1993, vol. xi, p. 53, note 292.

7 See J. Spencer Trimingham, *Christianity among the Arabs in Pre-Islamic Times*, Beirut, Longman, 1979, *passim*. I gratefully acknowledge my indebtedness to this noted scholar. There is extensive literature on this subject, largely inaccessible, and he has been masterly in making its findings available to a wider readership.

8 Samuel Hugh Moffett, *A History of Christianity in Asia*, San Francisco, Harper, 1992, vol. i, p. 338. See also Hitti, *History of the Arabs,* p. 105 who says that this was the case even in the first century after Muḥammad.

9 Ya'qūbi, History, vol. I, p. 298 quoted Trimingham, *Christianity among the Arabs in Pre-Islamic Times,* p. 263. See also p. 260.

10 Ibn Ishaq, in the edition of ibn Hisham: *As-Sira an-Nabawiyyah*, Beirut, Lebanon, Dar Ehia al-Tourath al-Arabi, Rue Dakkkache, undated, in 4 vols, vol. 3, p. 56.

11 See https://mmabbasi.com/2010/02/20/malaysias-youngest-mufti-

get-rid-of-banned-words-for-non-muslims/.

12 i.e. Latin *Anno Hegirae* –'in the year of the Hijra'.

13 Trimingham, *Christianity among the Arabs in Pre-Islamic Times*, pp. 51, 55, 56–8.

14 St Jerome regarded Philip as the first Christian emperor: 'qui primus de regibus Romanis Christianus fuit.' See his *De Viris Illustribus*, 54.

15 Sidney H. Griffith, *The Bible in Arabic*, Princeton University Press, 2013, p. 116.

16 *Hagarism: The Making of the Islamic World*, Crone, Patricia & Cook, Michael, Cambridge University Press, 1977, p. 3.; http://dev.worldpossible.org:81/wikipedia_en_all_2016-02/A/Early_Quranic_manuscripts.html; https://www.gawaher.com/topic/740824-what-is-the-oldest-complete-quran/.

17 Vatican Arabic MS 13.

18 Griffith, *The Bible in Arabic,* p. 127.

19 Vatican Arabic MS 17.

20 http://www.arabicbible.com/arabic-bible/codex.html?showall=1.

21 Cf. scanned copy of first page of the Epistle to the Hebrews, in *Mt Sinai Arabic Codex 151*. See note 9.

22 Trimingham, *Christianity among the Arabs in Pre-Islamic Times*, p. 295. Also J. Ryckmans, *La persécution des Chrétiens Himyarites aux sixième siècle*, 1956, p. 7.

23 Ibn Ishaq, in ibn Hisham: *As-Sira an-Nabawiyyah*, vol. 1, p. 29. See also *The History of al-Tabari*, vol. v, p. 206 and note 512.

24 The numbering of the Psalms reflects the difference between the ancient Septuagint or Greek text followed by St Jerome and the Eastern and Western Catholic Church from the earliest days of Christianity, and the Masoretic or Hebrew text followed by most Protestant translators. Scholars agree that psalms 9 and 10 in the Hebrew were one acrostic poem, wrongly divided into two. Psalm 78 refers to the Hebrew text, and [77] refers to the Greek text.

25 Michael McDonald, quoted Rick Brown, 'Who was Allāh before

Islam? (1)', *The Micah Mandate*, 19 October 2007, pp. 9–10.

26 www.islamic-awareness.org/history/islam/inscriptions/zebed.html.

27 Alfred Guillaume, *Islam*, Penguin, 1982, p. 10.

28 Hitti, *History of the Arabs,* p. 101.

29 *Deities and Dolphins: The Story of the Nabataeans*, New York, Farrer, Straus & Giroux, 1965, p. 527.

30 Ibid., p. 119, note 48.

31 Trimingham, *Christianity among the Arabs in Pre-Islamic Times*, pp. 65–6.

32 Francis Dvornik, *Francis Byzantium and the Roman primacy,* Fordham University Press, 1966, p. 47.

33 Trimingham, *Christianity among the Arabs in Pre-Islamic Times*, p. 83.

34 Ibid., p. 118.

35 N. S. Gill, www.thoughtco.com/greek-language-in-byzantine-empire-118733.

36 Samuel Hugh Moffett, *A History of Christianity in Asia*, San Francisco, Harper, 1992, p. 275.

37 Ibid., pp. 273–4; Trimingham, *Christianity among the Arabs in Pre-Islamic Times*, pp. 96–100.

38 'De S. Moyse, Episcopo Saracenorum in Arabia', *Acta Sanctorum*, Bollandists ed. 1657, Tomus 5, ii February, pp. 43–5.

39 Trimingham, *Christianity among the Arabs in Pre-Islamic Times*, p. 99, note 18.

Chapter 2

1 Virgil, *Georgics,* Book II, line 534.

2 Marcus Tullius Cicero, *Oratio IV in Catilinam*, vi. see M. Tullii Ciceronis *Opera Omnia*, ed. Carolus Fridericus Augustinus Nobbe, London, David Nutt, 1850, p. 429.

3 *If… it had Happened Otherwise,* ed. J. C. Squire, London, Longmans, Green and Co, 1932, pp. 21ff; 49 ff. Maurois was the pen-name of Emile Herzog, 1885–1967.

4 Reinhart Dozy, *Spanish Islam*, London, Chatto & Windus, 1913 p. 68

5 Edward Gibbon, *The History of the Decline and Fall of the Roman Empire,* London Ward, Lock & Co., undated, vol. ii, p. 254.

6 Trimingham, *Christianity among the Arabs in Pre-Islamic Times,* pp. 185–8.

7 *The History of al-Tabari*, vol. v, p. 355.

8 Ibid., p. 359. See also Trimingham, *Christianity among the Arabs in Pre-Islamic Times*, p. 200.

9 2 Samuel 11,1.

10 Hitti, *History of the Arabs,* pp. 264–5.

11 H. Daniel-Rops, *The Church in the Dark Ages*, London, J. M. Dent and Sons, 1959, pp. 315–16.

12 Ibid., p. 316.

13 *Sic, The History of al-Tabari*, vol. 5, p. 398; Gibbon, *The History of the Decline and Fall of the Roman Empire*, p. 280 says 'eighteen'. Other sources read 'twenty-four' or 'fifteen'.

14 *The History of al-Tabari*, vol. 5, pp. 396–8.

15 Ibid., p. 399. See note 984 where the Byzantine historian Theophanes claims that Kavad II was poisoned by his step-mother Shirin, quoting A Christensen, *L'Iran sous les Sassanides*, 2nd enlarged edn. Copenhagen, 1944, p. 497, note 1.

16 Ibid., p. 402, note 991.

17 Ibid., pp. 404–5 records a tradition that would have the Holy Cross returned by Būrān, daughter of Khosrau II who was the third successor as ruler of Ctesiphon after the death of her brother Kavad II. She reigned for one year and four months.

18 *Plutarch's Lives*, by John and William Langhorne, London, Ward, Lock & Co., undated, 'Pyrrhus,' p. 284.

19 Daniel-Rops, *The Church in the Dark Ages*, p. 317.

20 Jumada 1, AH [after the Hijra] 8.

21 Ibn Ishaq, in ibn Hisham: *As-Sira an-Nabawiyyah,* vol. 4, pp. 25–6. See also pp. 20ff. Cf. also David Margoliouth, *Mohammed*

and the Rise of Islam, New York, Cosimo Classics, 2006, p. 377.

22 Margoliouth, *Mohammed and the Rise of Islam*, p. 377.

23 Ibid.

24 Hitti, *History of the Arabs*, p. 147.

25 Ibn Ishaq, in ibn Hisham: *As-Sira an-Nabawiyyah*, vol. 4, p. 30.

26 Hitti, *History of the Arabs*, p. 152.

Chapter 3

1 Hitti, *History of the Arabs*, p. 142.

2 *The History of al-Tabari*, vol. vi, p. 132. 'Abd al-Malik Ibn Hishām, in his *al-Sirah al-nabawiyyah*, Beirut, Lebanon, Dar Ehia al-Tourath al-Arabi, Rue Dakkkache, 4 vols, vol. 2, p. 54, says that there were 73 men and 2 women.

3 See *Kitab al-Tabaqat al-Kabir*, by Ibn Sa'd, vol. i, lx.

4 At this time, before Muḥammad's conquest of Mecca, there were still three hundred and sixty-five pagan idols in the Ka'aba.

5 Walid Shoebat, 'ISIS will take over the most dangerous Muslim nation on earth,' shoebat.com, 24 November 2014

6 Actually the deputation was made up of people from the Khazraj and Aws tribes. It was customary to refer to the *'Ansar,'* or 'helpers' as the supporters of Muḥammad from Medina were called, as 'Khazraj,' probably because it was the most powerful tribe.

7 *The History of al-Tabarī*, vol. vi, pp. 133–4.

8 *Al-Bukhari, Sahih, Medina al-Munawwara, Dar Ahya as-Sunnah al Nabawiya*, undated, 9 vols, vol. 3 cap. i, # 874. 'He never touched the hand of any women while taking their pledge of allegiance and he never took their pledge of allegiance except by his words only'.

9 This was true of the age of which we write. Later, *sadaqah* became a 'voluntary' alms tax that was exacted from Muslims.

10 *The History of al-Tabarī*, vol. ix, pp. 47ff. See also David Margoliouth, *Mohammed and the Rise of Islam*, reprint: New York, Cosimo Classics, original edition 1905, pp. 418ff.

11 Dozy, *Spanish Islam*, pp. 18–19. See also *The History of al-Tabarī*, vol. ix, p. 45, note 239, 'The delegation asked that they be exempted from several other things, such as the interdictions on adultery, usury and wine.'

12 He is said to have scourged his son to death for drunkenness and immorality. See Ḥusayn ibn Muḥammad Diyarbakri, 1558 or 1559: *Ta'rīkh Al-khamīs,* Cairo edn., 1302 A.H. [1884 A.D] quoted Hitti, *History of the Arabs*, p. 176.

13 Dozy, *Spanish Islam,* p. 19, note 1.

14 See Richard Burton, *The Book of the Thousand Nights and A Night*, Burton Club, London, 1885, 18 vols., vol. 2, p. 158, note 2. See also p. 159, note 1.

15 David S. Margoliouth, *The Early Development of Mohammedanism, The Hibbert Lectures*, 2nd Series, 1913, reprint: Simon Publications Inc., 2003, pp. 58–9.

16 Some sources read 'goat'.

17 *The History of al-Tabarī*, vol. viii, pp. 123–4.

18 A non-Muslim subject living in a Muslim country.

19 *The History of al-Tabarī*, vol. x, pp. 1–18; Bertold Spuler, *The Muslim World* Part I,' The Age of the Caliphs,' p. 18.

20 See J.H. Kramers, *Analecta Orientalia*, Leiden, E. J. Brill, 1956, vol. ii, p. 226

21 *The History of al-Tabarī*, vol. x, p. 5

22 Ibid., p. 3

23 *Tarīkh al-Tabarī*, Beirut, Dar Ibn Hazim, 2005, 2 vols, vol. 1, p. 860.

24 *The History of Al-Tabarī*, vol. x, pp. 5–8.

25 Ibid., p. 11.

Chapter 4

1 *The History of al-Tabari*, vol. v, p. 41: 'From every tribe either a small part or the whole showed disobedience and apostatized'.

2 Al-Bukhari, *Sahih*, Medina al-Munawwara, Dar Ahya as-Sunnah

al Nabawiya, undated, 9 vols, vol. 9, chapter xxii, # 37, p. 26.

3 Ibid., p. 27.

4 *Tarīkh al-Tabarī*, vol. i, p. 873.

5 *The History of al-Tabari*, vol. x, p. 131.

6 Dozy, *Spanish Islam*, p. 22.

7 Daniel-Rops, *The Church in the Dark Ages*, p. 333.

8 Albert Hourani, *A History of the Arab Peoples*, London, Faber and Faber, 1981, pp. 22–3.

9 John Renard, *Responses to 101 Questions on Islam*, New York, Paulist Press, 1998, #9, p. 14.

10 *Encyclopaedia of Islam*, Leiden, Brill, 1960, vol. 1, p. 728.

11 *The History of al-Tabari*, vol. x, p. 28, note 172.

12 *Tarīkh al-Tabarī*, vol. i, p. 890.

13 Ibid., p. 876. See also *The History of al-Tabarī*, vol. x, p. 57

14 *The History of al-Tabarī*, vol. x, p. 74.

15 Ibid., vol. ix, pp. 106–7.

16 Dozy, *Spanish Islam*, pp. 22–3.

Chapter 5

1 Hitti, *History of the Arabs*, pp. 144–5.

2 The first four Caliphs of Medina (632–661), the Umayyid Caliphs of Damascus (661–750), and the Abbasid Caliphs in Baghdad (750–1258).

3 Al-Baladhuri took his name from a memory-enhancing drug called *Baladhur* that killed him.

4 *The History of al-Tabarī,* vol. xii, pp. 79, 80; *Tarīkh al-Tabarī*, vol. 1, p. 1029, trans. Paul Stenhouse.

5 Cf. *Annals Australasia,* 5/2015.

6 *The History of al-Tabarī,* vol. x, p. 41; *Tarīkh al-Tabarī*, vol. 1, p. 872, trans. Paul Stenhouse.

7 *The History of al-Tabarī,* vol. x, p. 14; *Tarīkh al-Tabarī*, vol. 1, p.

863, trans. Paul Stenhouse.

8 *The History of al-Tabarī*, vol. xii, pp. 79, 80; *Tarīkh al-Tabarī*, vol. 1, p. 1029, trans. Paul Stenhouse.

9 *The History of al-Tabarī*, vol. x, p. 177. *Tarīkh al-Tabarī*, vol. 1, p. 918.

10 Hitti, *History of the Arabs*, p. 159.

11 *The History of al-Tabarī*, vol. x, pp. 100–1; *Tarīkh al-Tabarī*, vol. 1, p. 890.

12 *The History of al-Tabarī*, vol. xii, pp. 75, 80; *Tarīkh al-Tabarī*, vol. 1, pp. 1026, 1029.

13 I assume that this refers to millions of gold dinars. The Arabs before this did not usually deal in gold. Though Mecca's trade was estimated to be worth 300,000 gold pounds when Muḥammad took it in 629 according to Albert Guillaume, *Islam*, Penguin, 1954, p. 42. During the Khalifate of 'Umar the weight of 10 dirhams is estimated to have been equivalent to 7 dinars, i.e. one mithqal or 4.25 grams. See www.sunnahmoney.com/gold-dinar-silver-dirham/.

14 Dozy, *Spanish Islam*, p. 123, and see pp. 110–12.

15 Ibid.

16 *The History of al-Tabarī*, vol. xii, p. 74; *Tarīkh al-Tabarī*, vol. 1, p. 1027.

17 *The History of al Tabarī*, vol. xii, p. 80; *Tarīkh al Tabarī*, vol. 1, p. 1029.

18 *The History of al-Tabarī*, vol. xii, pp. 76–7.

19 Ibid., p. 80; *Tarīkh al-Tabarī*, vol. 1, p. 1029

20 Hitti, *History of the Arabs*, p. 158

21 Trimingham, *Christianity among the Arabs in Pre-Islamic Times*, p. 118.

22 Michael Winter, *Saint Peter and the Popes*, London, Darton Longman and Todd, 1960, p. 185.

23 See Al-Baladhuri, *Kitab Futuh al-Buldān*, translated by Philip Khuri Hitti, Columbia University, 1916 (reprint Gorgias Press, 2002), p. 187.

Chapter 6

1 Some sources say that Damascus fell in 634. Hitti, *History of the Arabs*, p. 150, favours 635.

2 Ibid.

3 Al-Baladhuri, *Kitab Futuh al-Buldān*, pp. 186ff.

4 Ibid., p. 187.

5 *The History of al-Tabari*, vol. vii, p. 85.

6 Hitti, *History of the Arabs*, p. 104.

7 'Ali Dashti, *23 Years: A Study of the Prophetic Career of Mohammad*, New York, Mazda Publications, 1994, p. 87.

8 Ibid., p. 88.

9 *The History of al-Tabari*, vol. viii, p. 85.

10 Ibid., pp. 85–7.

11 See *The Life of Muhammad* by Ibn Ishaq, trans. A. Guillaume, Karachi, OUP, 2001, pp. 367–9. See also entry under *Ka'b bin al-Ashraf*, by W. Montgomery-Watt, in *Encyclopaedia of Islam*, vol. iv, p. 315.

12 *The History of al-Tabari*, vol. viii, pp. 156ff.

13 See 'Ali Dashti, *23 Years*, p. 90; and Hitti, *History of the Arabs*, p. 117. *The History of al-Tabari*, vol. viii, pp. 14–15 describes how one Jew, Ka'b bin Asad, but not the Banu Kuraiza as such, broke the treaty with Muḥammad; and pp. 23–5ff describe how Muḥammad played the Banu Kuraiza and the Quraish and their allies, against one another: tempting the former to break the treaty, and tricking the latter into calling off the siege.

14 See 'Ali Dashti, *23 Years*, p. 90.

15 See Q33[26–27].

16 *The History of al-Tabari*, vol. viii, p. 35.

17 *Tarīkh al-Tabarī*, vol. 1, p. 700.

18 'ISIS smuggler: We will use refugee Crisis to infiltrate West,' *WND*, 9 May 2015; see also *UNHCR Refugees Daily*, 17 June 2015.

19 Hitti, *History of the Arabs*, pp. 285–90.

20 Samir Khalil Samir SJ, *111 Questions on Islam*, San Francisco, Ignatius Press, 2002, p. 66.

Chapter 7

1 John Esposito, *Islam: the Straight Path*, New York, OUP, 2011, 4th edn., p. 64.

2 See Kevin Donnelly, 'School Textbooks gloss over jihad and undermine Christianity,' *The Australian*, 28 March 2015.

3 http://www.arabicbible.com/arabic-bible/codex.html?showall=1.

4 This article restricts itself to a brief discussion of these claims and counter claims.

5 Hitti, *History of the Arabs*, pp. 144–5. For an over view of this period, see Daniel-Rops, *The Church in the Dark Ages*, pp. 332–624; and Horace Mann, *The Lives of the Popes in the Early Middle Ages*, Kegan, Paul, Trench, Trubner & Co, London 1903, vols. i–vii.

6 Daniel-Rops, *The Church in the Dark Ages*, p. 369.

7 Sources differ concerning Yazdagird's age, the place of his death, and its circumstances. See Baladhuri, *Kitāb Futūh al-Buldān*, trans. Philip Hitti, Gorgias ed. 2002, pp. 490–3; also Gibbon, *The History of the Decline and Fall of the Roman Empire*, vol. ii, pp. 479–80. For a more complete list of alternative versions of Yazdagird's death see *The History of al-Tabari*, vol. xv, trans. R. Stephen Humphreys, pp. 78 ff. According to the *Chronicle of Theophanes, Anni Mundi 6095–6305 (a.d. 602–813)*, trans. Harry Turtledove, Philadelphia, Pennsylvania Press, 1982, p. 40, Mesopotamia fell in 633.

8 *Chronicle of Theophanes*, p. 39

9 Daniel-Rops, *The Church in the Dark Ages*, p. 336.

10 Hitti, *History of the Arabs*, p. 167.

11 Ibid.

12 Gibbon, *The History of the Decline and Fall of the Roman Empire*, vol. ii, pp. 539 ff.

13 Hitti, *History of the Arabs*, p. 501

14 The term 'Saracen' is sometimes mistakenly derived from the Arabic *Sharqi* or 'Easterner'. St Jerome (Ezek. viii, 25) considered it to be the name the Arabs gave themselves, deriving their origins from Sarah, Abraham's free wife, rather than from Hagar, his slave; we concur. In many of the sources we have used, the term 'Agareni', or 'Hagarines,' is found.

15 Letter from Adelbert, Marquis of Tuscany and protector of the Papal territory of Corsica, to Pope Sergius II in *Liber Pontificalis*, n. xliv, ed. Farnesiana.

16 Daniel-Rops, *The Church in the Dark Ages*, p. 472.

17 Quoted Steven Runciman, *A History of the Crusades*, Cambridge University Press, 1951, vol. i, p. 43.

18 See Mann, *The Lives of the Popes in the Early Middle Ages*, vol. iii, p. 321.

19 Jacques-Paul Migne, Patrologia Latina, tome 126, Epistle cccxxxiv – fragment of a letter to the Emperor.

20 Ibid., Epistle ccxcvi – to the Byzantine Emperor Basil, 12 August 880.

21 Mann, *The Lives of the Popes in the Early Middle Ages*, vol. iv, p. 10.

22 Flodoard (894–966), *Chronique de France 919–966*, entry for 921.

23 Daniel-Rops, *The Church in the Dark Ages*, pp. 340, 344.

24 Register of Gregory VII, III, 19.

25 H. Daniel-Rops, *Cathedral and Crusade*, J.M.Dent and Sons, London, 1957, p. 434.

26 Runciman, *A History of the Crusades*, vol. i, p. 105.

Chapter 8

1 *Sun Daily*, 21 August 2008.

2 'The Malaysian government is seen as being complicit in endorsing the rise of radicalism for its political manoeuvring and expediency':

Rafizi Ramli, Malaysian Opposition Treasury Spokesman, in 'Malaysian MPs urge Australia to do more to stamp out extremism,' *The Guardian,* 21 October 2014.

3 Elliot Brennan, 'Malaysia's ISIS Problem', *The Interpreter*, 30 October 2014.

4 Shannon Teoh, 'ISIS eyes Malaysia's pool of professional talent,' *Straits Times*, 22 October 2014.

5 Joshua Kurlantzick, 'Malaysia's Growing Climate of Repression gets Ignored,' *The Diplomat*, 25 October 2014.

6 'Malaysian Lawyers march against sedition law,' *Nation*, 17 October 2014.

7 Shurā (شورى) is Arabic for 'consultation,' 'deliberation'. The concept is often adduced as a proof that Islam can be 'democratic'.

8 'Group of Prominent Malays calls for rational dialogue on position of Islam in Malaysia,' *Nation,* 7 December 2014.

9 Kate Mayberry, 'Catholic Church "Allah" appeal shot down in Malaysia,' *Al-Jazeera,* 21 January 2015. Also 'Malaysian Court rules use of "Allah" exclusive to Muslims,' ABC, 14 October 2013.

10 'Malaysian Court restricts use of "Allah" to Muslims,' *The Hindu,* 14 October 2013.

11 Jim Khong, 'Malaysian court rules only Muslims can use Allah,' *Catholic Answers Forum,* 30 June 2014.

12 Celine Fernandez, Call for Religious Leaders to teach Acceptance in Malaysia, *The Wall Street Journal*, Asia edn., 7 January 2014.

13 Manirajan Ramasamy, Pooi Koon Chong, Andrea Tan, 'Malaysia Catholics can't use Allah as religious strife rises,' *Bloomberg Business*, 21 January 2015.

14 Melissa Goh, 'Najib stirs up controversy with UMNO–ISIS comment,' ChannelNewsAsia, 24 June 2014.

15 Teoh, 'ISIS eyes Malaysia's pool of professional talent'.

16 Brennan, 'Malaysia's ISIS Problem'.

17 Ibid.

18 'Another Malaysian Jihadist allegedly killed in Syrian Ambush,' *Malaymailonline,* 10 September 2014.

19 Farik Zolkepli, 'Leader of Aussie Terror Cell Nabbed,' *Nation*, 16 January 2015.

20 Laura Smith-Spark, 'UN rights chief slams global "paralysis",' CNN, 22 August 2014.

21 John Hall, 'The Growing Influence of ISIS,' *Daily Mail Australia*, 15 October 2014.

22 Walid Shoebat, 'ISIS will take over the most dangerous Muslim nation on earth,' Shoebat.com, 24 November 2014.

23 Teoh, 'ISIS eyes Malaysia's pool of professional talent'.

Chapter 9

1 Justin Worland, 'Pope Francis Condemns ISIS killing of Coptic Christians,' *Time*, 16 February 2015.

2 Woodrow Wilson Centre, 'Muslims Against ISIS'.

3 Dana Ford et al., CNN News, 6 January 2015.

4 On 24 September 2014.

5 http://www.reddit.com/r/exmuslim/comments/2p5lyc/criticising_the_criticism_of_isis_from_120/. See also: Ayman S. Ibrahim, 'Muslim Scholars vs. ISIS,' *First Things,* 3 October 2014.

6 See Arabic text: http://www.lettertobaghdadi.com/pdf/Booklet-Arabic.pdf, section 9, p. 13.

7 See English text: http://www.lettertobaghdadi.com/14/english-v14.pdf, section 8, p. 8.

8 Ibid., section 7, p. 6.

9 Ibid., section 10, p. 11.

10 Ibid., section 8, p. 7.

11 Ibid.

12 'Abd al-Rahman abu-Zaid ibn Khaldun, *The Muqaddimah, an Introduction to History,* trans. by Franz Rosenthal, Bollingen Series xliii, Princeton University Press, 1980, 3 vols., vol. 1, ch. iii,

section 31, p. 473.

13 Ibid., p. 480.

14 Al-Bukhārī, *Sahīh,* Medina al-Munawwara, Dar Ahya us-Sunnah al Nabawīya, 9 vols., vol. 4, 386, p. 255.

15 http://www.usc.edu/org/cmje/religious-texts/hadith/muslim/019-smt.php#019.4294.

16 This is Philip Hitti's suggested translation of the much disputed عن يد in Q9[29]. See his *History of the Arabs*, p. 144.

17 Q9[29].

18 English text quoted note 5, section 4, p. 5.

19 See Ibn Ishaq (Ibn Hisham), *Biography of Muhammad*, Arabic version, Beirut, Lebanon, Dar Ehia al-Tourath al-Arabi, Rue Dakkache, 2000, 4 vols, vol. 4, p. 248 line 6: امره ان يدعوهم الى الاسلام قبل ان يقاتلهم.

20 Ibid., pp. 248–50. Trans. Paul Stenhouse.

21 *Tarīkh al-Tabarī*, vol. 1, p. 876. Trans. Paul Stenhouse.

22 'Muhajirun': those Muslims who fled from Mecca to Medina with Muḥammad.

23 'Ansar' – the 'helpers,' the Medinese tribesmen who 'supported' and 'helped' Muḥammad.

24 *The History of al-Tabari*, vol. x, p. 57.

25 *Tarīkh al-Tabarī*, vol. 1, p. 876. Trans. Paul Stenhouse.

26 Muḥammad Mahmoud Rabi', *The Political Theory of Ibn Khaldun*, Leiden, EJ Brill, 1967, pp. 52, 169.

27 *Cf.* Woodrow Wilson Centre, 'Muslims Against ISIS'.

Chapter 10

1 Apostolic Exhortation, *Ecclesia in Europa*, 2003.

2 'Relativism, Christianity and the West,' Joseph Ratzinger and Marcello Pera, *Without Roots*, New York, Basic Books, 2006, p. 44. *Mutatis mutandis,* I have made my own the words of Marcello Pera.

3 *Truth and Tolerance*, San Francisco, Ignatius Press, 2004, Preface.

4 Ratzinger and Pera, *Without Roots*, p. 45.

5 After World War II the US recognized West Germany after four years, and restored diplomatic relations after ten years, in 1955. Diplomatic relations were restored with Tokyo after seven years, in 1952.

6 Elise Labott, 'Kerry reassures Gulf allies in talks on Iran, Syria,' CNN, 23 January 2016.

7 Iran was supposed to be behind the majority Shia uprising in 2011 in Bahrain. An independent body set up by the king found this could not be unsubstantiated. Iran has never hidden its support for the Alawites and other minorities in Syria. A pity the Christian West didn't feel the same way about Christian minorities.

8 *Telegraph*, London, 14 January 2015.

9 Labott, 'Kerry reassures Gulf allies in talks on Iran, Syria'.

10 *Kingmakers*, Karl E. Meyer & Shareen Blair Brysac, New York, W.W.Norton & Company, 2008, p. 227.

11 Ibid.

12 Tony Katon, 'Condi in Diplomatic Disneyland,' *Time*, 26 July 2006.

13 'How Hezbollah Defeated Israel,' Alistair Crooke, Mark Perry, *Asia Times*, 12 October 2006. 'Israel lost the war in the first three days,' one US military expert said.

14 Katon, 'Condi in Diplomatic Disneyland'.

15 Dr Mohammad Salim al-Rawashdeh and Dr Hani Abdulkareem Akho Rshaidah, 'The future of Arab Spring: reality and ambition,' *Global Journal of Interdisciplinary Social Sciences,* July–August 2014, p. 136.

16 Seth Jones, 'The Mirage of the Arab Spring,' *Foreign Affairs*, Jan./ Feb. 2013.

17 http://english.alarabiya.net/en/News/middle-east/2016/01/24/ Kerry-reassures-Saudi-Arabia-of-solid-relationship-.html.

18 George Weigel, 'Foreword' to Ratzinger and Pera, *Without Roots*, p. ix.

19 *The Turkish Letters of Ogier Ghiselin de Busbecq, Imperial Ambassador at Constantinople 1554–1562*, trans. from the Latin by Edward Seymour Forster Oxford, 1927, p. 112.

20 C. T. Forster and F. H. B. Daniel, eds., *The Life and Letters of Ogier Ghiselin de Busbecq, vol. I* (London: Kegan Paul, 1881), *passim* but see pp. 86–8, 153–5, 219–22, 287–90, 293.

21 Ratzinger and Pera, *Without Roots*, pp. 4, 5.

22 *Why we should call ourselves Christians – the Religious roots of Free Societies*, Preface by Pope Benedict XVI, New York, Encounter Books, 2011.

23 St Luke, xi, 24–6.

24 'Ali Dashti, *23 Years*, p. 207.

25 Christopher Catherwood, *Churchill's Folly: How Winston Churchill Created Modern Iraq*, New York, Carrol & Graf, 2004, p. 87 quoted *Kingmakers*, p. 160.

26 See Ratzinger and Pera, *Without Roots*, p. 42.

Chapter 11

1 http://www.thereligionofpeace.com/pages/quran/violence.aspx; accessed 17 April 2016.

2 See Muslims vs. 'Outlaws of Islam': Islamic Voices Lead Fight Against Extremists, by Peter Jesserer Smith, *National Catholic Register*, 6 January 2016.

3 Gerard Henderson, 'Think murder and then call it poetry,' *Sydney Morning Herald*, 9 March 2004.

4 Letter dated 28 November 1985 from Lebanese Moslem Association referred to by Jackson J. in *Minister for Immigration and Ethnic Affairs v Lebanese Moslem Association & Ors* (1987) 17 FCR 373 at 386.

5 Ibid.

6 Hans Wehr, *A Dictionary of Modern Written Arabic*, ed. J. Milton Cowan, Wiesbaden: Otto Harrassowitz, 1971, p. 425

7 *Annals Australasia,* 9/10 2015, pp. 36–40.

8 Ibid., p. 37.

9 *The Second Message of Islam*, Mahmoud Mohammed Taha, trans. Abdullahi Ahmed an-Na'im, Introduction, New York, Syracuse University Press, 1987, p. 37. I have drawn on the work of Abdullahi Ahmed an-Na'im, for Mahmoud's thought and doctrine.

10 Ibid., *passim*, especially pp. 124–45.

11 Ibid., p. 37.

12 *The Political Philosophy of Jacques Maritain,* eds. Joseph Evans and Leo Ward, New York, Image books, 1965, p. 278.

Chapter 12

1 See *Erga kai Hemerai*, or 'Works and Days,' a poem by the Greek poet Hesiod, written c.700 BC.

2 Abu al-Fath, *Kitab al-Tarikh*, ed. and trans. Paul Stenhouse, Sydney, Mandelbaum Press, 1985, p. 28.

3 Shakespeare, *Julius Caesar,* Act iii, scene 1, line 273.

4 Prologue to *Henry V.*

5 See Robert Gates, *From the Shadows*, New York, Simon and Schuster, 2006.

6 Steve Coll, 'Anatomy of a Victory: CIA's covert Afghan War,' *Washington Post*, 20 July 1992, quoted Charles Cogan, 'Partners in Time: the CIA and Afghanistan since 1979,' *World Policy Journal,* summer 1993, p. 76.

7 *Le Nouvel Observateur*, 15–21 January 1998. Since 2014 the newspaper has been known as *L'Obs.*

8 Hassan Abbas, *The Taliban Revival: Violence and Extremism on the Pakistan-Afghanistan Frontier*, 2014, Yale University Press, p. 67. Quoted: Wikipedia: Jamiat Ulema-e-Islam.

9 See al-Jazeera, 29 October 2004 at 21.00 GMT.

10 Andrew Hartman, '"The Red Template": US policy in Soviet-

occupied Afghanistan', *Third World Quarterly*, 23/3 2002, p. 485.

11 Ahmad Rashid, 'The Taliban: Exporting Extremism', *Foreign Affairs*, Nov./Dec. 1999, pp. 22–35.

12 Ibid.

13 'The Wilder Shores of Politics,' *International Journal*, 37/winter 1981–82, p. 7.

14 'Foreign Affairs; Angry, Wired and Deadly', *New York Times*, 22 August 1998.

15 *Messages to the World*, ed. Bruce Lawrence, 2005 Verso, London and New York, p. 175.

16 Ibid. passim.

17 Jonathan Steele, '10 Myths about Afghanistan,' *The Guardian*, 28 September 2011.

18 Rashid, 'The Taliban: Exporting Extremism'.

19 Hartman, 'The Red Template', p. 471.

20 Ibid.

21 *Le Nouvel Observateur*, 15–21 January 1998.

22 *The Guardian*, 16 June 2017.

23 http://nchv.org/index.php/news/media/background_and_statistics/.

24 Bruce McDougall, 'Australia's shame as destitute war veterans are homeless and alone,' *Daily Telegraph*, 9 November 2015. See Marija Jovanovic, 'More Australian soldiers lost to suicide than fighting in Afghanistan War,' SBS, 30 November 2016.

Chapter 13

1 *A History of Greece*, London, John Murray, 1869, 12 vols, vol. 1, p. 86, note 1.

2 Oliver Burkeman, 'US Firms get $1.5bn deal to rebuild Iraq,' *The Guardian*, 18 March 2003.

3 Seth Kline, 'The Other Symbol of George W. Bush's Legacy,' *US News and World Report*, 12 May 2003.

4 Brad Hoff, 'New declassified CIA Memo Presents Blueprint for Syrian Regime Collapse,' *The Liberterian Institute*, 14 February 2017.

5 Ibid.

6 Garrett Epps, 'Trump's Unlawful Attack in Syria,' *Atlantic,* 9 April 2017.

7 Molly Hennessy-Fiske and Nabih Bulos, 'Syrians Report 15 dead in US airstrike,' *Los Angeles Times*, 7 April 2017.

8 Figures quoted range from 281 (French Intelligence) to 1729 (Free Syrian Army).

9 Jerome R. Corsi, 'Evidence: Syria gas attack work of US allies,' WND Exclusive, 26 August 2013.

10 Ariella Phillips, 'Trumps 2013 tweets to Obama: "Do not attack Syria",' *Washington Examiner,* 6 April 2017.

11 Corsi, 'Evidence: Syria gas attack work of US allies'.

12 Patrick J. McDonnell, 'Syria's Assad denies use of chemical weapons,' *Los Angeles Times*, 26 August 2013.

13 Ibid.

14 Shaun Waterman, 'Syrian rebels used Sarin nerve gas, not Assad's regime: UN Official, *Washington Times*, 6 May 2013.

15 'Top Former US Military and Intelligence Figures: Trump should Rethink Syrian Escalation', *Washingtonsblog*, 11 April 2017. See https://consortiumnews.com/2017/04/11/trump-should-rethink-syria-escalation/.

16 Ibid.

Chapter 14

1 'Idjtihad,' *Encyclopaedia of Islam*, vol. iii, pp. 1026–7.

2 See Samir, *111 Questions on Islam*, p. 43.

3 https://www.youtube.com/watch?v=huMu8ihDlVA.

4 See Mark Curtis and Nafeez Ahmed, 'The Manchester Bombing as Blowback: the Latest Evidence', *World News Daily*, 3 June 2017.

5 Dan Bilefsky and Rick Gladstone, 'Insidious Twist in Terror

Attack Victims,' *New York Times*, 23 May 2017.

6 https://au.news.yahoo.com/a/35632786/manchester-bombing-australian-muslim-leaders-clash-over-terrorists-motive/#page1.

7 Chloe Patton, 'Welcome to the Weird World of Australia's 'Fake Sheikh' Mohammad Tawhidi,' *ABC Religion and Ethics*, 11 April 2017.

8 Samir, *111 Questions on Islam*, p. 66.

9 Dozy, *Spanish Islam*, pp. 239–40. For 'Omar's 'blunt statement' quoted by Dozy, see Abu Isma'il al-Basri, *Futuh ash-Sha'm*, p. 124. Also see R. Dozy, *Histoire des Musulmans d'Espagne*, E. Lévi-Provençal, Leyde, E.J. Brill, 1932, tome I, p. 283.

10 'Gunmen in Egypt force Coptic Christians from buses and kill 28,' *New York Times*, 26 May 2017.

11 http://www.abc.net.au/news/2017-06-01/will-the-afghan-attack-affect-donald-trumps-troops-decision/8578072.

12 'Australian Zaynb Al Harbeya, 12, killed in terrorist bombing,' *News.com.au*, 31 May 2017.

13 Samir, *111 Questions on Islam*, p. 71.

14 Jacqeline Hole, 'Muslim Group wants sharia law in Australia,' *ABC News* 17 May 2011.

15 Judith Bergman, 'Sharia Down Under', *The Gatestone Institute*, 29 May 2017.

16 Stephen Johnson, 'Muslim leader Keysar Trad says an angry husband can beat his wife but should use his fists as a last resort …' *Daily Mail Australia*, 23 February 2017. See also *Herald Sun* Melbourne, Andrew Bolt, 18 April 2017.

17 A.F.L. Beeston, *Baidawi's Commentary on Surah 12 of the Qur'an*, Oxford, Clarendon Press, 1963, pp. 47–8.

18 Ibid., p. 73, note 160.

19 *An Arabic English Lexicon,* Williams and Norgate, London, 1877, Book 1, Part 6, p. 2449.

20 The famous Qāmūs (lexicon) dating from 1277, which formed the basis of Lane's own Lexicon.

21 'Tafsīr,' *Encyclopaedia of Islam*.

22 Al-Bukhari, *Sahih*, Medina al-Munawwara, Dar Ahya us-Sunnah al-Nabawiya, undated, 9 vols, vol. 1, #301. See also vol. 3, #826.

23 *Encyclopaedia of the Qur'an*, Jane Dammen McAuliffe, gen. ed., Brill, Leiden, 2006, vol. 5, p. 524.

Chapter 15

1 David Wroe, 'Bourke Street attack: Scott Morrison demands Muslim leaders "call this out for what it is",' *Sydney Morning Herald*, 10 November 2018.

2 'PM calls out extremist, violent, extremist Islam', 9NEWS.

3 'Bourke Street attack: Scott Morrison slammed for Islam remarks,' *The Australian*, 10 November 2018.

4 Melissa Davey, 'Bourke Street attack: Morrison accused of "scapegoating" Muslim Community,' *The Guardian*, 12 November 2018.

5 Fares Hassan, Nick Baker, 'Australia's Grand Mufti rejects government calls to do more to combat extremism,' *SBS News*.

6 Ibid.

7 Ibid.

8 'Bourke Street attack: Scott Morrison slammed for Islam remarks'.

9 See 'The Antechamber of Islamic Fundamentalism,' *Annals Australasia*, 2/2018, p. 31.

10 See Mahmoud Mohamed Taha, *The Second Message of Islam*, Abdullahi Ahmed An-Na'im, Syracuse University Press, 1987, *passim*.

11 Ibid. See also, for example, Amnesty International, 8 April 1995, Human Rights Commission of Pakistan p. 82 of its Annual Report 1995. Also 'Plight of Ahmadi Muslims in Pakistan (1899–1999)', p. 43. All non-Sunni minorities as well as moderate, non-radicalised Sunnis, are in danger from radical Sunni extremists.

12 See, 'Pakistan delays release of Christian woman after blasphemy

acquittal,' *CBS News,* 2 November 2018.

13 Ibid.

14 Ramon Taylor, 'NYC Ahmadiyya Muslims hit with double discrimination,' *VOA*, 15 April 2018.

15 See, Adam Coogle, 'Anti-Shia Bias Driving Saudia Arabia Unrest', *Human Rights Watch,* 24 August 2017. Uzay Bulut, 'Persecution of Alevis in Turkey,' 18 January 2018, *Gatestone Institute.* Nile Green, 'Why ISIS hates the Sufis and blows up their shrines,' *Aeon,* https://aeon.co/ideas/could-sufism-offer-an-alternative-to-isis-for-young-muslims, *passim.*

16 *Middle East Institute*, 'Salafism and the Persecution of Shi'ites in Malaysia.'

17 Rania El Rajji, 'Even War discriminates,' Yemen's Minorities, exiled at home, in *Briefing*, Minority Rights Group International, *passim.*

18 *Encyclopaedia of the Qur'an*, vol. 1, 345–7; vol. 5, 412–15 and *passim.* See also Chris Moore, 'The Burqa – Islamic or cultural?' http://www.quran-islam.org/articles/part_3/the_burqa_(P1357).html. See also Mahmoud Mohamed Taha, *The Second Message of Islam, passim.*

19 *Reuters*, 3 December 1996. Quoted Michael Griffin, *Reaping the Whirlwind, The Taliban Movement in Afghanistan,* London, Pluto Press, 2001, p. 168.

20 Moha Ennaji, 'Why Morocco's burqa ban is more than just a security measure,' *The Conversation,* 1 February 2017.

21 Ed Husain, *The House of Islam: A Global History*, Bloomsbury 2018, p. 280.

www.ingramcontent.com/pod-product-compliance
Ingram Content Group Australia Pty Ltd
76 Discovery Rd, Dandenong South VIC 3175, AU
AUHW020136130726
429791AU00003B/103